PURIFYING
the
HEART

For Jianne
Much metta
Mary Jo

PURIFYING
the
HEART

Buddhist Insight
Meditation for Christians

Kevin G. Culligan
Mary Jo Meadow
Daniel Chowning

CROSSROAD · NEW YORK

1994

The Crossroad Publishing Company
370 Lexington Avenue, New York, NY 10017

Printed in the United States of America

Library of Congress Cataloging-in-Publication Data

Culligan, Kevin G.
    Purifying the heart: Buddhist meditation for Christians / by
Kevin G. Culligan, Mary Jo Meadow, Daniel Chowning.
        p.   cm.
    Includes bibliographical references.
    ISBN 0-8245-1420-3
    1. Contemplation. 2. Meditation—Catholic Church. 3. Meditation—
Buddhism. 4. Vipaśyanā (Buddhism) 5. Carmelites—Spiritual life.
6. John of the Cross, Saint, 1542–1591. 7. Catholic Church—
Doctrines.   I. Meadow, Mary Jo, 1936– . II. Chowning, Daniel.
III. Title.
BV5091.C7C85   1994
248.3'4–dc20
                                                            94-19319
                                                               CIP

*To our Silence and Awareness retreatants,
who have inspired and encouraged us*

Blessed are the pure in heart,
for they shall see God.

—Matthew 5:8

When you are cleansed of all impurity
and the stain of all sinful passions is gone,
you can enter the blessed abode of the saints.

—The Dhammapada, no. 236

Contents

Part III
THREE LEVELS OF PURIFICATION:
ST. JOHN OF THE CROSS AND
THERAVADAN BUDDHISM COMPARED

Section One
The First Level of Purification
CONDUCT

Section Two
The Second Level of Purification
MENTAL CONTENTS

Section Three
The Third Level of Purification
FRUITION

Part IV
QUESTIONS CHRISTIANS ASK

PREFACE

This book is addressed to Christians who long for the happiness of seeing God that Jesus promised to the pure in heart. By offering an ancient Buddhist meditation practice within a Christian prayer tradition, we hope to teach our readers a process of inner purification that we believe can lead to deeper Christian faith in this world and the direct vision of God in the next.

Eastern Riches for Christians

We write primarily for Christians with at least some interest or experience in Eastern meditation. Despite the long history of mysticism within Christianity and its many and varied approaches to meditation and contemplative prayer, more and more Christians during the last twenty-five years have turned to Eastern religions to find guidance for their interior life that they did not find in Christianity. Some have completely abandoned the religion of their childhood, believing they have found the "pearl of great price" (Mt 13:45–46) in Eastern meditation.

Others have discovered for themselves Christianity's rich mystical tradition. They have set out on their own to build a bridge between their Eastern meditation practice and Christian contemplative prayer. Such persons, who often call themselves Buddhist Christians (or Christian Buddhists), draw equally upon both traditions to assist their interior development and growth in Christian faith.

Still other Christians have experienced the physiological and psychological benefits of meditation practices drawn principally from Eastern sources, although they are uncertain how to relate meditation to their faith. They are open to integrating their meditation practice into their Christian life if someone can show them how. Many worry about syncretism in their religious practice or fear becoming New Age dilettantes, believing it safer to keep religion and meditation separate.

We cannot know how many Christians have at least some experience with Eastern meditation, but we suspect there are many. This book offers them reliable guidance for integrating at least one form of Buddhist meditation into one tradition of Christian contemplative prayer.

The Silence and Awareness Retreat

We write this book especially for the benefit of those who have made the eight-day Silence and Awareness retreat, which we have directed since 1989, and of those who have worked privately with the Credence Cassettes tapes of our 1991 retreat. In this retreat, we teach the Theravadan Buddhist practice of *vipassana*, or insight meditation, within the framework of Christian contemplative prayer found in the tradition of Carmelite spirituality, especially in the life and writings of St. John of the Cross.

As we developed this retreat from year to year, we gradually recognized the need for this book. We want to make the basic instructions for insight meditation available in writing for those who have made this retreat in person or through audiotapes to use when they work with this practice on their own. We also want to set down, as clearly and simply as possible, our understanding of how this ancient Buddhist practice can be integrated into Christian prayer.

Our intent in this book is thus primarily pastoral and practical. We recognize, but do not intend to discuss, the many important questions that occupy professional scholars in the Buddhist-Christian dialogue and in the study of

Christian spirituality. We are also aware of, but do not intend to elaborate, the social and political implications of collaboration between persons of differing religious faiths. We intend simply to teach the practice of Christian insight meditation, providing only as much history and theory as seems necessary to show the compatibility of this simple Buddhist practice with Christian prayer. We believe that Christians who are faithful to this practice soon discover for themselves its power to bring inner peace and healing, its implications for Christian life, and the inseparable connection between wisdom and compassion known for centuries to both Christian and Buddhist meditators.

Plan of the Book

Part I briefly lays the foundations of our approach. We first present Jesus' call to purity of heart. Next we give a historical outline of the Buddhist tradition of insight meditation and the Carmelite tradition of prayer. Then we recap our own work in drawing from the Gospel and these two venerable traditions a contemplative practice we call Christian insight meditation.

Having laid this historical foundation, we give in Part II the instructions for insight meditation as they are taught during our retreats. This enables the reader to learn and experience the meditation practice directly. In Part III, we compare the teachings of St. John of the Cross and the Buddha on interior purification. This comparison provides the primary theoretical basis for our effort to integrate insight meditation into Christian prayer. Finally, in Part IV, we respond to the questions our retreatants most often ask about using insight meditation as prayer.

Because insight meditation focuses on self-emptying purification, we only briefly describe the Buddhist loving-kindness meditation practice. However, in her book, *Gentling the Heart: Buddhist Loving-Kindness Practice for Christians,* our coauthor, Mary Jo Meadow, teaches this practice in detail. Together, our two books show both the interior and social implications of Theravadan Buddhism for Christian spirituality.

Vatican II

In writing this book we have been guided by the spirit of the Second Vatican Council, which exhorts Catholic Christians to "acknowledge, preserve and promote" the spiritual and moral goods and cultural values of Hinduism and Buddhism (Declaration on the Relationship of the Church to Non-Christian Religions [*Nostra Aetate*], no. 2). Vatican II also challenges missionary members of religious institutes to reflect attentively "on how Christian religious life may be able to assimilate the ascetic and contemplative traditions whose seeds were sometimes already planted by God in ancient cultures prior to the preaching of the Gospel" (Decree on the Church's Missionary Activity [*Ad Gentes*], no. 18).

We have tried to be as faithful as possible to the integrity of both Buddhist insight meditation and Carmelite spirituality. At the same time, we attempt to point out the similarities between these two traditions that enable us as Catholic Christians to "assimilate" Buddhist insight meditation into Christian prayer and to teach an authentic Christian insight meditation.

We deeply believe that the Christian insight meditation taught in this book, a twenty-five-hundred-year-old Buddhist meditation practice integrated into Carmel's eight-century tradition of contemplative prayer, can satisfy the hunger of American Christians for spiritual nourishment. This growing spiritual hunger is one of the most pressing pastoral challenges of the American Church. To satisfy this hunger, we offer a meditation practice that not only purifies our hearts, but also draws us directly into the paschal mystery, the self-emptying death of Jesus Christ that gives new life to our world.

Emptiness is a common theme in the spiritual teachings of both the Buddha and John of the Cross. Emptying our lives of attachment to everything contrary to God's will and opposed to the free movement of the Holy Spirit within us is the essential process that prepares us for God's loving and transforming action in our lives. By fostering this emptiness, by leading us securely along a lifelong path of poverty of spirit and purity of heart, Christian insight meditation disposes us for this unfathomable blessing that alone satisfies all our longings.

In presenting Christian insight meditation, we recognize that we are latecomers in demonstrating the relevance of Eastern meditation for Christian prayer. Here we express our gratitude for Bede Griffiths, Thomas Merton, Abhishiktananda, John Main, Sister Ishpriya, Hugo Enomiya-Lassalle, William Johnston, Pascaline Coff, Yves Raguin, Raimundo Panikkar, Anthony de Mello, and many other pioneers in the field of ecumenical spirituality upon whose work we stand. You will easily discern their inspiration in our pages. However, because we want to capture in this book the atmosphere of our Silence and Awareness retreat in both the meditation instructions and spiritual conferences, we provide notes for only direct quotations in the text. All our other sources are included in the general bibliography.

Terminology

A word about terminology. Because of its non-discursive and passive nature, meditation in Buddhism has been likened to contemplation in Christianity. However, Carmelites, especially John of the Cross, generally regard contemplation as the inflow of God into the human person, a gift of God's love that we cannot achieve by our human actions alone. We can use various ascetical techniques and spiritual practices to dispose ourselves for contemplation, but the increase of divine life in us is always grace, God's gift.

To avoid confusion, we reserve the term "contemplation"

in this book to refer only to this grace. We use the words
"contemplative prayer" (or synonyms like "contemplative
practice" or "contemplative method") for the non-discursive
meditation practices we use to dispose ourselves for this gift
of contemplation. We will discuss the concepts of meditation,
contemplative prayer, and contemplation in greater detail in
Part IV. Until then, when we speak of contemplation, we
mean God's unmerited gift; when we speak of contemplative
prayer, we mean meditative practices that dispose us for that
grace.

Another word about authorship. Three persons have written this book. We have done our best to give you a smooth-
reading and consistent text, both in style and content. Because you will undoubtedly notice differences in our chapters, we have placed our initials at the end of our respective
chapters for your information.

Acknowledgments

Finally, words of thanks. We are grateful to Clarence Thom-
son, director of Credence Cassettes, and Michael Leach,
publisher of the Crossroad Publishing Company, for their
interest in our work and their encouragement to share our
retreat with a larger audience through audiotapes and this
book. We thank, too, John Eagleson, our editor at Crossroad, for his assistance in bringing this book to press.

We are especially grateful to Joseph Goldstein, Buddhist
author and cofounder and guiding teacher at Insight Meditation Society in Barre, Massachusetts, and Kieran Kavanaugh,
O.C.D., a founding member of the Institute of Carmelite
Studies and American translator of St. John of the Cross,
for their critical reading of our first draft and helpful com-
ments. They have both contributed immensely to this book,
although the authors alone are responsible for its final
form.

Finally, we thank all who have joined us for our Silence
and Awareness retreats. Their longing for genuine spiritual-

ity, their openness to our teaching and guidance, and their constructive criticisms of our work have made it possible for us now to share this experience with a wider audience. To these men and women, our retreatants, we dedicate this book.

K.C.

Credits

We gratefully acknowledge the following for permission to reprint previously published material:

ICS Publications for excerpts from *The Collected Works of St. John of the Cross,* translated by Kieran Kavanaugh and Otilio Rodriguez © 1979, 1991, by Washington Province of the Discalced Carmelites. ICS Publications, 2131 Lincoln Road, Northeast, Washington, DC 20002, U.S.A.

Scripture quotations not translated directly by the authors from original sources are taken from the following translations:

The New American Bible in *The Catholic Study Bible*. Edited by Donald Senior, Mary Ann Getty, Carroll Stuhlmueller, and John J. Collins. New York: Oxford University Press, 1990.

The Jerusalem Bible. Alexander Jones, General Editor. Garden City, N.Y.: Doubleday & Company, Inc., 1966.

The Revised Standard Version in *The R.S.V. Interlinear Greek-English New Testament* by Alfred Marshall. Grand Rapids, Mich.: Zondervan Publishing House, 1968.

Citations of St. John of the Cross

All quotations from John of the Cross are from *The Collected Works of St. John of the Cross,* rev. ed., trans. Kieran Kavanaugh, O.C.D., and Otilio Rodriguez, O.C.D. (Washington, D.C.: ICS Publications, 1991), sometimes with a change of wording for the sake of meaning or inclusive language. References cite book, chapter, and paragraph, without the page number. References appear after the quotation in the text rather than in the end notes. In these references, A=*The Ascent of Mount Carmel,* N=*The Dark Night,* C=*The Spiritual Canticle,* F=*The Living Flame of Love,* L=Letters.

Part I

Foundations

Chapter 1

PURITY OF HEART
The Teaching and Example of Jesus

"Blessed are the pure in heart," Jesus teaches in his Sermon on the Mount, "for they shall see God" (Mt 5:8). For Jesus, the heart is more than the bodily organ that sustains physical life; it is the interior center of our being from which all life flows. The New Testament depicts the heart primarily as the source of our feelings, desires, and passions, of our thoughts and understanding, of our will and its choices, of our moral and religious behavior.[1] Accordingly, Jesus teaches that we must purify our entire interior life if we want the happiness of seeing God.

Jesus Demands Purity of Heart

That Jesus demands such inner purity is clear from his challenge to the Pharisees about ritual purification. "Listen to me, all of you," he said, "and understand. Nothing entering from outside causes a person to be unclean; rather it is what comes out of the person that makes for uncleanness." Jesus later explained to his close disciples that ritual food leaves the heart unaffected. It simply passes through the body into the sewer. All foods, therefore, are clean. However, persons become unclean by what comes out of them. "For it is from within, from the heart, that evil intentions emerge: fornication, theft, murder, adultery, avarice, malice, deceit, indecency, envy, slander, pride, folly. All these evils come

23

from within. They make a person unclean" (Mt 15:10–20; Mk 7:14–23).

To see God, our hearts must be pure, free of all evil. God is holy and only the holy can rejoice in the divine presence. We cannot live before God with a heart filled with evil, with murder, deceit, envy, pride. We must first purify our hearts — our desires, thoughts, memories, emotions, and choices — of everything that might cause evil behavior. As we gradually purify our interior life, we begin to know the happiness, the blessing, the joy of seeing God.

In this world, seeing God does not mean physical vision, but experiencing God in the events of our daily lives. It is knowing God in dark faith and constant love. Yet experiencing God in faith and love in this world leads, as the Apostle John assures us, to seeing God directly in the life beyond this world. "Beloved, we are already God's children," writes John in his first epistle, "although what we are to be in the future has not yet been revealed. However, we know that when he appears we shall be like him, for we shall see him as he really is. And those who thus hope in him purify themselves as he is pure" (1 Jn 3:2–3). Our true happiness in this world consists in embracing the purity of life we see in the teachings and example of Jesus, trusting that we shall be totally transformed in him when we finally see him face to face.

The Beatitudes

This happiness, Jesus reminds us, belongs not only to the pure of heart, but also to the poor in spirit, the gentle, the merciful, peacemakers, and those who mourn, who long for holiness, and who suffer persecution for his sake (Mt 5:3–10). His teaching on happiness implies a connection between all these ways of being in the world. The pure of heart are also poor in spirit. Just as no one who is pure of heart can be a murderer, an adulterer, or a liar, so the truly pure in heart also work for peace, show mercy, and strive for holiness. These are the qualities that bring us true happiness.

The happiness Jesus proclaims is thus paradoxical. The things we naturally expect to make us happy — money, prestige, power, security, pleasure — make us very unhappy when they become our only desire and close our heart to God. Purity, meekness, and simplicity, on the other hand, bring happiness because they cleanse our heart and open it for God, who alone makes us completely happy.

The kingdom of God, therefore, belongs only to the poor in spirit, the meek, the mourners, the peacemakers, the persecuted, to those who make room in their lives for God. There is no other way to establish the reign of God in our hearts.

Jesus, of course, does not expect us to purify our hearts by our own efforts alone. He knows too well what is in us (Jn 2:25). He knows especially our hardness of heart, our sclerocardia, to put it in medical terms. Of all human diseases, sclerocardia is the worst, worse even than cancer or AIDS, because it closes us to the Word of God and isolates us from God's love. We can be so absorbed in our own plans, desires, pleasures, thoughts, memories, and emotions that we exclude God from our hearts. As the divine physician who comes to heal us, Jesus' primary focus is to cure the hardness of heart that prevents the growth within us of faith, hope, and love and excludes the transforming power of God's love from our lives (Mt 8:5–15; Mk 6:5–6).

Death to Self

To heal our hardness of heart, Jesus calls us to die with him. "Those who want to follow me must renounce themselves, take up their cross, and follow me. Those who want to save their life must lose it; those who lose their life for my sake, and for the sake of the Gospel, save it. What gain is it to win the whole world and ruin one's life? And, indeed, what can one offer in exchange for one's life?" (Mk 8:34–38). As Christian discipleship demands death to self, so too does purity of heart. We cannot achieve the purity Jesus taught in the Sermon on the Mount unless we die interiorly.

We die interiorly every time we refuse to let evil intentions and movements of rage, envy, lust, injustice, avarice, pride, and slander take root in our consciousness, not allowing them a place in our hearts. As these movements pass through us, the heart's natural purity and simplicity emerges, grows stronger, and prepares us to experience God in new and un-suspected ways. After a lifetime of dying daily to disordered internal movements, we one day die finally into the complete, never-ending, unchanging presence of God.

Jesus exemplified his teaching with his own death on the cross. Although public preaching, teaching, healing, and community building were essential to his ministry, Jesus es-tablished God's reign in the world primarily through his death and resurrection. Similarly, his reign becomes estab-lished in our hearts as we daily share his death and resurrec-tion. There is no other way. "Unless a grain of wheat falls into the ground and dies, it remains just a single grain of wheat; but if it dies, it bears much fruit" (Jn 12:24).

Recognizing the good that comes to the human family through Jesus' death and resurrection, St. Paul increasingly emphasized union with Jesus in his paschal mystery — his dying and rising — as central to Christian living. In his letter to the Christians at Philippi, Paul challenged them in these words:

> In your minds
> you must be the same as Jesus Christ:
> His state was divine,
> yet he did not cling
> to his equality with God
> but emptied himself
> to assume the condition of a slave,
> and became as all human beings are;
> and being as all humans are,
> he was humbler yet,
> even to accepting death,
> death on a cross.

But God raised him high
and gave him the name
which is above all other names
so that all beings
in the heavens, on earth and in the underworld,
should bend the knee at the name of Jesus
and that every tongue should acclaim
Jesus Christ as Lord,
to the glory of God the Father. (Ph 2:5–11)

Speaking for himself, Paul went on to assure the Philippians of his own commitment to the paschal mystery: "All I want is to know Christ and the power of his resurrection and to share his sufferings by reproducing the pattern of his death. That is the way I can hope to take my place in the resurrection of the dead" (Ph 3:10–11).

We assume the mind of Christ when we embrace the process by which Jesus emptied himself for the human family in his suffering and death on the cross. His self-emptying was not a denial or renunciation of his unique personhood, but non-attachment to the divine honor and glory he could rightly claim. Jesus thus entered freely and completely into the depths of human suffering. The Father did not abandon Jesus in his self-emptying, but raised him from the dead and restored him to eternal glory. Now all creation praises and honors him as Lord. Similarly, purity of heart involves a self-emptying that does not destroy our personhood; rather, it opens us to the fullness of life as we share the Spirit of the Risen Lord who is given to us (Rm 5:5).

The Holy Spirit purifies us interiorly for God. As we cannot pray without the help of the Holy Spirit (Rm 8:26–30), neither can we purify our hearts without the Spirit's assistance. "You know perfectly well," Paul reminds the Corinthians, "that people who do wrong will not inherit the kingdom of God: people of immoral lives, idolaters, adulterers,...these are the sort of people some of you were once, but now you have been washed clean and sanctified, and justified through the name of the Lord Jesus Christ and through the Spirit of our God" (1 Cor 6:9–11). The Holy Spirit within us continually supports our efforts to put to death the self-indulgent passions and desires that cause our disordered behavior; moreover, the Spirit produces in our conduct the enduring fruits of interior freedom — love, joy, peace, patience, kindness, goodness, trustfulness, gentleness, and self-control (Ga 5:16–26).

Thus, we imitate Jesus in his self-emptying, not as an ascetical practice for its own sake, but because it purifies our heart and opens for us the door to freedom, love, peace, and life everlasting. This is the mystery of Christian faith. This is our daily rhythm of life. Indeed, purity of heart, poverty of spirit, mortification, non-attachment, and self-emptying not only lead to eternal life; they are eternal life already possessed, a risen life under the Holy Spirit's constant guidance lived here and now in this world, a life that promises joyous completion in the eternal vision of God.

Purity of heart, then, is like the little mustard seed in Jesus' story that grows from a very small seed to a large bush providing shelter for the birds of the air (Mk 4:30–32). It is a hidden and humble activity, yet it brings us every blessing — — happiness, Gospel living, healing and transformation in Christ Jesus, the gifts of the Holy Spirit, eternal life. These permit us to experience God now in faith and to see God later in heaven.

Purifying the Heart

But how, precisely, do we purify our hearts? First, by our love for Jesus. Our hearts become pure as we listen to his words, practice his teaching, follow his example, and, most importantly, die daily to self-love in union with his death on the cross.

We can also learn from others. Long before the time of Jesus, the Old Testament psalmist prayed: "A clean heart create for me, O God, and a steadfast spirit renew within me"

(Ps 51:12). Like this ancient poet, we can purify our hearts by humbly asking God each day for this blessing in our lives.

In addition to prayer, we can learn the ancient practices of the pure in heart. Following his own enlightenment around the year 500 B.C.E., the holy man of India, Gotama, the Buddha, taught his followers the importance of purifying the heart by abandoning evil and doing good. He stated: "When you are cleansed of all impurity and the stain of all sinful passions is gone, you can enter the blessed abode of the saints."[2]

Meditation, he taught them further, is the practice that cleanses the heart. It purifies the heart of disordered desires, hateful thoughts, harmful memories, fear and other negative emotions, and, in their place, engenders sharp mental awareness, clear understanding, strength of will, and attentiveness to each passing moment. It develops wisdom and compassion, and finally opens one to ultimate truth, unconditioned being, or *nibbana*. Over the centuries, the Buddha's followers have preserved their meditation practices with such care and precision that they are now available to all who wish to use them in response to Jesus' call to purify the heart.

Christians, too, have developed effective methods for purifying the heart. The sixteenth-century Spanish Carmelite friar St. John of the Cross meticulously describes in *The Ascent of Mount Carmel* and *The Dark Night* the progressive interior purification necessary for union of the entire person with God. He gives counsel on how to systematically purify desires, thoughts, memories, and emotions so that the heart may be disposed to receive God's love in contemplation. Contemplation purifies, heals, and, ultimately, transforms the entire human personality, both sense and spirit, and unites it with God.

John teaches that only God's love for us fully purifies our hearts and unites us perfectly with God's will. Divine love makes us God by participation, enables us to experience God in this life through faith, and after death to see God and live forever in God's presence. Nevertheless, through the faithful practice of meditation and continual recollection, we can attain a purity of heart, a poverty of spirit, and an emptiness of self that irresistibly invites God into our lives and frees us to receive God's purifying and transforming love in contemplation.

The chapters that follow in this book bring these two venerable traditions — Buddhist meditation and the Christian spirituality of St. John of the Cross — together into an ascetical practice we call Christian insight meditation. This contemporary approach to purifying our hearts lets us know, as Jesus promised, the happiness of seeing God, first in this world by dark faith, then by direct vision in eternity. This practice aims, in the spirit of the Beloved Disciple's first epistle, to help Christians purify themselves as Jesus is pure, so that their hope of seeing him and being finally transformed in him may be fulfilled (1 Jn 3:2–3).

Before explaining Christian insight meditation further, let us look first at brief historical overviews of the Buddhist tradition of insight meditation and the Carmelite tradition of prayer.

K.C.

Chapter 2

THE BUDDHIST TRADITION
OF INSIGHT MEDITATION

Gotama, the Buddha, was born into a princely family about 500 B.C.E. in an area of India now part of Nepal. His father arranged a very sheltered life for him because he strongly wanted his son to be an important worldly leader. However, stories from the child's young life indicate that he was bound for future spiritual greatness. When he finally came into contact with the human suffering of illness, aging, and death, the young prince resolved upon a spiritual life. He left his palace and sought a spiritual teacher. Several teachers taught him all they knew, but he remained unsatisfied.

The *bodhisattwa* (Buddha-to-be) then spent years trying in various ways to break through to his goal of full, clear seeing of spiritual truth. Finally he hit upon the method of awareness practice. Various temptations of lust, greed, fear, and self-importance then launched a massive assault on him. After he overcame the final temptation, self-doubt, his enlightenment unfolded over an entire night during his thirty-fifth year, and he came to full understanding.

From this time on, he was known as the Buddha, or "The Fully Enlightened One." This fulfilled his vow made many lifetimes earlier to become a Buddha for the good of humankind. He then lived a long life of teaching and healing, and performed many miracles. His dying concern was with the well-being and spiritual illumination of his followers. He exhorted them to remember that all worldly things end and to work out their salvation diligently.

The Basic Teachings of the Buddha

The Buddha said that he taught one thing, and one thing only: suffering and the end of suffering. This emphasis on suffering is not pessimistic; the great point of the Buddha's teaching is that suffering *can* be overcome, that there is a way out that frees us from suffering.

Four noble truths.   In his first sermon after enlightenment, the Buddha taught the four noble truths that form his core message. The first noble truth is about suffering, only some of which is evident pain or hardship. He said that our earthly lives themselves are ultimately unsatisfactory because they can give us no lasting, permanent, and true satisfaction. We also must put great effort into passing and fleeting outcomes. Eventually aging, illness, and death come to all of us.

The second noble truth is the cause of suffering: craving. Whenever we have a pleasant experience or see the possibility of one, we tend to react with greed in the mind. Those who have wrestled with addictions probably best understand the suffering that craving brings. However, all of us who have something we feel we cannot live without — a person, a job, a possession — know the truth that craving means suffering.

Whenever we are faced with unpleasant experience, we want to strike out at it; we push it away, become fearful or angry, or grieve over it. This also is craving, wanting things to change. We feel driven to say the hateful word, shrink away from a frightening duty, or indulge in self-pity.

Whenever our experiences do not grip us strongly, we become careless, bored, or inattentive; we are "excitement junkies," and resist giving careful attention to routine details of life. This puts us in voluntary ignorance or delusion. Willingness to pay attention only to intense experiences is also craving.

The third noble truth is that suffering ends when we stop craving. When we no longer react to experiences with greed, aversion, and delusion, we no longer suffer. One meditator delightedly described her freedom from torment in a relationship. When faced with a co-worker who always annoyed her, she became aware of how unpleasant it was, but realized that she could choose not to react.

The fourth noble truth tells us how to end suffering by following the eightfold noble path. Traditionally, the path is broken into three main parts: morality, or purity of conduct; purity of mental contents; and wisdom, or purity of heart. Each of these frees us from some suffering and brings about a corresponding satisfaction.

Walking the path. The first task is to establish basic morality and purify behavior. Until this is done, we cannot know the happiness of freedom from guilt, remorse, and blame. When conduct is discordant, it brings suffering. It harms ourselves or others.

Purifying mental contents is the second task. Meditation practice works directly on this, by making us fully present and attentive. Then the practice can clear the mind of such remnants of psychological ill health as envy, resentment, greed, anger, vanity, and so on. When such thoughts no longer dominate mental contents, a second level of happiness comes. This calm, peace, and stillness of mind is the happiness of concentration, which leaves no room for the mental baggage that agitates us or may move us to unskillful action.

Finally, latent tendencies toward unwholesomeness cling to us, the results of past wrong choices we have made. The hidden inclinations they have left in our hearts can ripen into wrong thought or behavior with sufficient provocation. Because of impurity in the heart, we easily move to coveting and may even misbehave. Working with this is the deepest and most radical purification. Our task is simply to be present and let the work be done in us. The resulting purity of heart, when all that is unwholesome has been uprooted, finally brings the end of suffering. We enjoy the happiness of wisdom that culminates in experiencing the Ultimate Reality, which Buddhists call *nibbana*. Others call the Ultimate Reality such names as God, Brahman, the Absolute, Allah, Great Spirit, the Transcendent, or the Higher Power.

Three characteristics.   The Buddha taught that only *nibbana* is unconditioned — that is, unborn, undying, unchanging, and truly satisfying. Everything else is conditioned reality, dependent upon causes. Three types of conditioned reality exist in ourselves and the rest of the world: matter, consciousness, and mind-states. Our bodies are matter, and consciousness is the knowing faculty. Mind-states, which color experience, include moods, emotions, sets, and states of awareness.

Meditation practice shows us that all conditioned reality has three common characteristics. We have already discussed one, suffering or unsatisfactoriness. Another is that things are constantly changing; nothing lasts. Everything is continuously being born and passing away. We can see how rapidly our thoughts and emotions change; our bodies also constantly pass off dying cells and create new ones.

The third characteristic of all conditioned or created reality is essencelessness, or no-self. This is one of the Buddha's hardest teachings to understand. However, if we reflect, we realize that what we call ourselves is a combination of ever-changing processes of body and mind. It is not a solid and permanent "thing." Also our science of physics tells us that even the most solid-looking matter is mostly empty space with flecks of "stuff" floating in it. All that we know of this world is processes within larger processes, combinations of constantly changing processes. There are no static or permanent "things," just changing processes. This is what no-self means; nothing in conditioned reality lasts in any essential form. All is never-ending flux and flow.

Trappedness and freedom.   The Buddha taught that everything happens dependent on causes; every experience that arises is born from something else. He described laws of cause and effect in areas Western science recognizes, laws that say how matter, life forms, and mind work. His teaching on dependent arising explains another law, the law of moral cause and effect. This is about how we are trapped and unfree, and how we can become free.

The basic problem is that we are not willing to accept things as they are without unhelpful reacting to them, without craving. We are trapped in our reactions to experiences, and the suffering that brings, because of our past choices. We have conditioned ourselves into a prison from which awareness practice can release us.

This practice is beautifully summed up in one of the Buddha's shortest teachings. He simply said, "In seeing, let there be only what is seen; in hearing, let there be only what is heard; in sensing, let there be only what is sensed; in cognizing, let there be only what is cognized." The point is to be fully aware of our experience, without adding interpretation or commentary, without getting lost in it, clinging to it, or pushing it away. This means simply being with what is happening right now, being fully present to the moment. It means surrendered acceptance of "what is," whether agreeable to us or not. However, it does not mean passivity in the face of evil or when action is called for.

Awareness practice shows us our trappedness in clear detail. It is also our way out and actually works the needed purification in us. In freeing us from trappedness in conditioned reality, the practice brings the fruit of "touching" *nibbana,* the only true satisfaction.

Development of Buddhism

The Pali canon of Buddhist scriptures began in a meeting of monks shortly after the Buddha's death. Of the early Buddhism, based on the Pali canon, only the Theravadan school remains. Its stronghold is southeast Asia, in Burma, Thailand, and Sri Lanka. The awareness practice we teach is from a Burmese Theravadan school. Part II of this book gives you practice instructions.

Other Buddhist schools. What is now called Mahayana Buddhism began within centuries of the Buddha's death. These understandings traveled north into Tibet where they merged with Tibetan folk religion to become Tibetan Buddhism. This highly stylized and ritualistic Buddhism has a very deep meditative tradition. The larger Mahayana tradition developed as the Buddha's teachings went further north and east to China and, by way of Korea, to Japan. The Mahayana takes many forms, from Zen, which is very like Theravadan awareness practice, through groups emphasizing chanting or other rituals, to forms of "churched" Buddhism, influenced by Christian missionary activity.

In many forms, Buddhism is now a major world faith, found in all parts of the globe. However, the meditation practice itself is not considered a religion, but simply spiritual practice, often called *dhamma* practice.

Meditation writings of Buddhism. We now look at the twenty-five-hundred-year-old awareness practice, mindfulness practice, or insight meditation, in more detail. In the Pali language, this practice is called *vipassana* (pronounced vi-pahs'-suh-nuh), or clear, wide seeing through.

The Pali canon contains the Buddha's sermons (*suttas*) that describe his awareness practice. Most important is the *Mahasatipatthana Sutta*,[1] which fully details how to practice mindful awareness. Another large collection of early scriptures, the *Abhidhamma*,[2] contains Buddhist philosophical and psychological understandings. These depictions of human nature clearly explain our need for mindful awareness.

Apart from scriptures, the major work on Buddhist meditation is the fifth-century monk Buddhaghosa's *Visuddhimagga*, or *The Path of Purification*.[3] It details one thousand years of experiences of many thousands of meditators. It tells exactly what to expect at each stage of meditation practice from the signs that it is starting to those signaling its end. These fifteen-hundred-year-old Asian writings accurately describe our own experiences when we meditate in the twentieth-century Western world.

History of insight (*vipassana*) practice. For a long time insight meditation remained a monastic practice, because it was thought suitable only for monks and nuns who had dedicated their entire lives to spiritual practice. Early in the twentieth century, some monks began to teach the practice to lay Buddhists in southeast Asia. A chief figure in this was Burmese Mahasi Sayadaw, whose school is the most widespread in the West. He is also considered one of the great meditation masters of all time. Mahasi Sayadaw wrote extensively on insight practice, though most of his works are not yet available in English.[4]

By mid-century, Westerners were studying insight meditation in Asia. Some returned home and began teaching the practice. A major Western breakthrough was the founding in the mid-1970s of Insight Meditation Society in Barre, Massachusetts.[5] The books of Joseph Goldstein,[6] one of the IMS founders and a major teacher of the practice, are a good place to start reading about insight meditation. *Vipassana* practice is also available at some other Buddhist centers. With the 1987 founding of Resources for Ecumenical Spirituality,[7] sponsor of the authors' retreats, the practice became regularly available in the context of Christian Carmelite spirituality.

Understanding Insight Meditation

Nature of awareness practice. Insight meditation practice is rigorously empirical. Its profound psychology is based on practitioners' introspective accounts of their meditation experiences. Centuries of meditators described their experiences to knowledgeable teachers. These, in turn, monitored neophytes' progress, assessing it against what was already known about the practice. The result is a very precise and elaborate developmental psychology that has remained valid, accurate, and helpful over many centuries. Because wanting or expecting certain experiences might distort practice, teachers typically explain stages of meditation in detail only after students are already familiar with them in their own work.

The precise method is certainly one important feature of this practice. Equally important is its discouraging of metaphysical speculation. We need not agree with any belief items or be willing to call on any supernatural beings to do the practice. This makes the practice available to everyone without any conflict with whatever religious loyalties they have. The practice is simply a way to pay fine-grained, continuous awareness to all of our experiences of mind and body. Although it is this simple, it leads us to the highest stages of spiritual unfoldment as the major spiritual traditions, including St. John of the Cross, see them.

Fruits of practice.   Meditation practice helps us in many ways. Some of its fringe benefits are physical: lower blood pressure, lower resting pulse rate, relaxation, release of tension — even medical healings. It has healed many psychosomatic ailments, bodily ills that have a large emotional component. There are also directly emotional benefits: calming and clarifying emotions, and getting us in touch with emotions before they start to move us around. Mental benefits include better concentration, the ability to focus and stay focused, and freedom from fretting, stewing, worrying, and other mental wanderings that cause distress.

Buddhist insight meditation is primarily a purgative or purifying form of practice. It dredges up all our unfinished moral, emotional, mental, and even bodily experiences to purge and heal them and to unify the personality. This meditation practice reveals the depths of our own being to us and forces self-honesty on us. This can profoundly improve physical, emotional, and mental health. Some people use it as an alternative to psychotherapy.

However, spiritual benefits are the chief purpose of the practice, although those who practice for these other benefits do get them. The spiritual goal is the unmanifest Ultimate Reality, *nibbana*, the only unconditioned, unborn, undying, unmoving, unchanging reality. Insight practice directly prepares us for this. To "touch" *nibbana*, or to "know" God, requires a very deep purification of conduct, mental contents, and the heart. The purgatory of insight meditation practice leads to that purity of heart of which the beatitude says: "Blessed are the pure of heart, for they shall see God."

M.J.M.

Chapter 3

THE CARMELITE TRADITION OF PRAYER

Early Carmelite History and the Rule of St. Albert

The Carmelite tradition of prayer began around 1209 C.E. on Mount Carmel in the Holy Land. A group of laymen, most likely disillusioned crusaders from Europe, gathered as hermits near a spring named in honor of the Old Testament prophet Elijah to live in solitude and prayer after the example of the great prophet. Little is known about these Western hermits except that they petitioned Albert, the Patriarch of Jerusalem, to give them a rule of life. This rule, known as the Rule of St. Albert, embodies the earliest elements of Carmelite spirituality. The hermits were to live a common life committed to following Jesus Christ, serving him with "a pure heart and a good conscience." Sacred Scripture nourished their prayer life. They assembled daily for the communal celebration of the Eucharist and weekly for meetings to discuss their way of life.

The rule especially enjoined constant prayer in solitude, calling them "to meditate day and night on the Law of the Lord." In imitation of Jesus Christ, who retired alone on the mountain to pray, the hermits dedicated themselves to solitary unceasing prayer. In the Middle Ages, "meditation" on the Scriptures meant much more than reasoning, which is our usual understanding of the word. Meditation was a matter of the heart. It involved the constant repetition of a word

or phrase from Scripture, allowing those words to sink deep
into the heart to purify it of all that was not God.

For inspiration in their life of prayer, the hermits of Mount
Carmel looked especially to Mary, the mother of Jesus, and
to the prophet Elijah. Just as Mary allowed the Spirit of God
to possess her and thus gave birth to Jesus the Redeemer of
humanity, the early Carmelites strove to surrender themselves
completely to the Spirit of God to become vessels of Christ's
healing presence in a world marred by sin. The prophet Elijah represented for them a man totally dedicated to God who
walked zealously and lived continuously in the presence of
God. To imitate this fiery prophet, the hermits sought God
alone in all things. They endeavored to live with purity of
faith and to walk always in God's presence with unswerving
fidelity and love.

Carmelites in Europe

The Saracen invasion of Palestine in the middle of the thirteenth century ended the hermits' life of solitary prayer on
Mount Carmel. The Carmelites returned to Europe to establish their eremitical life there. This posed difficulties. No
longer could they survive in solitary places as they had in
the Holy Land. The change in culture and the ministerial
needs of the thirteenth century forced them to adapt their
lifestyle to new circumstances. Consequently, they included
more communal aspects in their rule and added an apostolic
dimension to their religious life. They became friars along
with the new emerging orders of mendicants such as the
Franciscans, Dominicans, and Augustinians.

The apostolic orientation of Carmelite life demanded serious theological study to prepare clerical friars for ministry.
By the end of the thirteenth century, the friars had entered the
great university movement begun earlier in the century and
established houses of study near the great educational centers of Europe. The intellectual life of the order flourished.
Carmelites were numbered among the renowned theologians,

spiritual writers, and humanists of the fourteenth and fif-teenth centuries.

However, the more active and academic life of the friars, together with the negative effects of the Black Plague, the Hundred Years War, and the Western Schism, led to a decline in the observance of the rule. This brought many attempts during the fourteenth and fifteenth centuries to restore bal-ance between the contemplative and active aspects of the Carmelite life and to recapture the original spirit of those first hermits on Mount Carmel.

The Carmelite Nuns and St. Teresa of Jesus

An important development of the order began in 1450. Pope Nicholas V signed a bull that permitted pious women to come under the protection of the Order of the Blessed Vir-gin Mary of Mount Carmel. Under the guidance of Blessed John Soreth, the general of the order, and Blessed Frances of Amboise, the Carmelite nuns blossomed and flourished throughout Europe. Their cloistered life dedicated to interior prayer and the public worship of God revitalized and deeply enriched the spirit of Carmel.

St. Teresa of Jesus entered one of those convents in Avila, Spain, in 1535. Teresa de Ahumada y Cepeda was born in 1515. She entered the Carmelite convent of the Incarnation when she was twenty years old and lived there for twenty-seven years. Those years were marked both by periods of mystical graces received through contemplative prayer and by inner conflict. For many years, Teresa resisted God's call to deeper fidelity.

When Teresa was thirty-nine years old, a profound conver-sion transformed her life. One day in prayer, she discovered the liberating love of the humanity of Jesus Christ, who freed her from the attachments that for almost twenty years had prevented her from giving herself more completely to God. As she grew freer, Teresa realized that contemplative prayer held the key to healing and transformation in her life.

Teresian Prayer

Teresa's conversion profoundly shaped her understanding of interior prayer. In her autobiography, Teresa defines prayer as "an intimate sharing between friends."[1] To pray is to enter into a loving relationship with Jesus Christ, who lives in the depths of our hearts. The more Teresa opened herself to God's love through contemplative prayer, the more she experienced herself loved by God, not just once, but many times, and at ever deeper levels of her being. This loving relationship healed her brokenness and purified her of the attachments and sinful patterns that had earlier prevented her from centering her life completely on God. Teresa thus came to see relationship as the essence of prayer. She discovered that prayer is a loving relationship that transforms because love alone heals and purifies the human person.

For Teresa, the experience of God was also an encounter with Jesus Christ. Her earliest method of prayer was to strive to remain present to Jesus Christ living within her.[2] As her relationship with Christ deepened, the Risen Lord revealed himself powerfully to her as a faithful friend and companion in life. He introduced her into the mystery of the Trinity. As a result, Teresa stressed the importance of the humanity of Jesus Christ in our relationship with God. In and through Jesus Christ, we learn who God is and what it means to be fully human. As our model and faithful friend, Jesus leads us to an ever deeper experience of our Triune God. Throughout her writings Teresa teaches her readers "to look" at Christ — within themselves, in the Gospels, in the Eucharist, and in one another.[3]

Finally, Teresa's prayer became increasingly interior and dynamic. As her contemplative life deepened, Teresa became more and more conscious of God's presence within her. In *The Interior Castle*, she writes that the "soul is like a castle made entirely out of a diamond or of very clear crystal, in which there are many rooms."[4] At the very center of this "castle" dwells God, who imparts to us life, beauty, and dignity. Prayer is the doorway through which we enter this "castle." The contemplative life is an interior journey into the very depths of our being where we meet our loving God. As our journey inward deepens, we become more conscious of God's dynamic presence within us and of our own life being rooted in Christ.

Yet, Teresa did not relegate interior prayer only to formal periods of solitude. She understood prayer as a way of life. Prayer and life go hand in hand. We are in relationship with God, not only when we are on our knees, but in every aspect of our lives. For this reason, Teresa emphasized the importance of constant growth in virtue as a foundation and expression of our relationship with God. She particularly stressed the virtues of love of neighbor, humility, and detachment. She knew from her own experience that mutual love and respect, truthfulness, and interior freedom are both necessary for contemplative living and fruits of its increase in our lives.

The Teresian Reform

Inspired by the primitive ideals of the first hermits on Mount Carmel and responding to the religious upheaval caused by the Reformation, Teresa began a reform convent of Carmelite nuns at San José in Avila in 1562. Her ideal in establishing this community was to gather a small group of women who would live as good friends of Christ and good friends of one another, all occupied in unceasing prayer for the good of the Church. Five years later, Teresa set out to establish other reformed communities throughout Spain.

In 1567, while making her second foundation of nuns in Medina del Campo, Teresa met a young Carmelite friar named John of St. Matthias. Previous to their encounter, John had been discerning his desire for a life of deeper solitude and prayer. Teresa persuaded him to join her reform. In 1568, John and another friar, with Teresa's assistance, established the first monastery of men in the Teresian Reform. At this time he changed his name to John of the Cross.

The friars shared the vision and charism of Teresa. They dedicated themselves to a life of contemplative prayer and public worship of God. However, unlike the nuns, who lived an enclosed religious life, the friars engaged in pastoral ministry. They preached in local parishes, taught catechism, heard confessions, and became renowned as spiritual directors. Their life of interior prayer, combined with public ministry, disposed them for a rich experience of God and of human nature that enabled them to assist others seeking a deeper relationship with God through prayer. John of the Cross, whose writings and example we follow in this book, became such a spiritual guide.

St. John of the Cross

John of the Cross was born of a poor family in 1542 in Fontiveros, Spain.[5] He entered the Carmelite friars in 1563 in Medina del Campo and was ordained in 1567. Writing out of his profound experience of God and human nature, John addressed his major works to the pastoral need for better spiritual guidance for his contemporaries. He showed persons a way of purifying and healing their hearts. In his ministry as confessor and spiritual director, John met many people whom God was inviting to deeper contemplative prayer but who felt confused and dismayed by their own interior poverty and darkness. Few spiritual directors seemed equipped to understand and discern the purifying movements of the Spirit in contemplative prayer. John desired to enlighten and encourage both spiritual people and their directors.

The starting point for understanding John of the Cross's spiritual teaching is our divine vocation to "union with God through love." God longs to be in relationship with us. We are created out of love and for love. By our very creation, God has destined us to participate fully through grace in the divine life of love and to love other persons and our world with God's own mind and heart.

However, a profound disorder exists in our relationships with God, others, and the world. Despite our best efforts, we find it difficult to love as God created us to love. Our human nature has been wounded by original sin, our past sinful choices, and our personal history with all the factors that make up our personality. We need healing and purification.

In *The Ascent of Mount Carmel* and *The Dark Night,* John analyzes the human condition and gives us a path toward healing. Our disordered relationships are seen in how we easily become enslaved by inordinate desires and attachments. We tend to pour out ourselves in created reality that will never fully satisfy us. We futilely seek peace and satisfaction of heart in material possessions, food, honors, unhealthy relationships, and even spiritual consolations in prayer. Our inability to love properly is present whenever self-gratification motivates our relationships with God, others, and creation. When we pray, help others, and fulfill our daily tasks solely for our own pleasure, we make our own ego the center of attention.

Contemplation: A Path of Purification

Sin and inordinate desires wound us so profoundly that we cannot heal ourselves. Only God's love can penetrate the deepest recesses of the human heart and purify its selfish desires and disordered relationships. John taught that contemplation, which he describes as a secret and peaceful inflow of God's love in the soul, heals the human heart of these disordered relationships. Contemplation is the fire of God's love that heals, purifies, and transforms our hearts, recreating them to reflect the image of God for whom we were created.[6]

John's symbol for this process of healing and purification is the dark night of the senses and the spirit. This night is both active and passive. In the active part, we undertake to purify ourselves out of love for God; in the passive part, God's love purifies, heals, and transforms us. Although we may experience the dark night as an absence of God or a time of painful self-knowledge and crisis, John believed that the dark night signals the dawn of new life. It is God's loving concern to restore and heal human nature.

The path of purification, John also taught, means following Jesus Christ. In *The Ascent of Mount Carmel,* John places before us the life and death of Jesus as the model of the path of purification.[7] Jesus lived a life of total dedication to his Father and of self-giving love for others that called for a total surrender of false securities and self-gratification. His death on the cross summarized his life of self-emptying love. Jesus performed his greatest work of salvation when he was most empty and poor on the cross. Following Jesus implies a life of loving dedication to God and the surrender of our attachments and selfishness in order to love more freely. It means becoming empty of self for the love of God and others in imitation of Jesus Christ.

Finally, John taught that the journey toward union with God means living the theological virtues of faith, hope, and love. These virtues both unite us to God and purify us. They are the way to union with God. God infuses the virtues into us and through them we enter into communication with God. Faith, hope, and love purify us by emptying the intellect, memory, and will of all that is not God. For John, the theological virtues are more than truths we assent to or actions we perform; they make possible our loving, interpersonal relationship with God that purifies our souls.

Subsequent Carmelite History

The Teresian Reform officially became an order separate from the Carmelites of the Ancient Observance in 1593. Known as Discalced Carmelite friars and nuns, the order spread rapidly throughout Europe. Even in Teresa's lifetime, mission efforts began in Africa. In 1790, Teresa's daughters came to the United States and made the first foundation of Discalced Carmelite nuns in Port Tobacco, Maryland. From 1209 to the present, Carmelites from both branches of the order have witnessed by their lives of prayer and apostolic zeal to the transformative power of prayer and the presence of the living God in our world. Among them are some of Christianity's great spiritual teachers. One example is St. Mary Magdalen de Pazzi in sixteenth-century Florence. From an early age, God graced Mary Magdalen with a profound insight into God's love for each individual and God's fidelity to us even in the midst of great interior darkness. She was known as an "angel of charity" because of her ardent love for God and others.

The seventeenth-century French lay brother, Brother Lawrence of the Resurrection, is widely known among Protestants and Catholics for his practice of the presence of God. This humble brother served his community as cook and sandalmaker and found God just as much among the pots and pans of his kitchen as when on his knees in chapel. His French Carmelite Sister, Elizabeth of the Trinity, announced a similar message in the twentieth century. Elizabeth based her spiritual life on the simple but profound truth that our Triune God dwells within the deepest recesses of our hearts. We possess all our riches within us. We need only allow the divine life within us to grow.

Another great French spiritual teacher of Carmel is St. Thérèse of Lisieux. Thérèse lived a hidden life of prayer and sacrifice, yet she is recognized as the Patroness of Missions and a genius of the spiritual life for her simple and refreshing Gospel message. Many people who experience their interior poverty and brokenness find an authentic path of transformation in her "little way" of confident surrender to God's merciful love.

Two great twentieth-century prophets of the Carmelite tradition of prayer are Blessed Titus Brandsma and Blessed Teresa Benedicta of the Cross (Edith Stein). Titus surrendered his life to God in 1942 in the Nazi death camp of

Dachau, and Teresa Benedicta sacrificed hers the same year in Auschwitz. In imitation of Jesus Christ, both offered their lives freely for the salvation of a world stigmatized by hatred and violence. They proclaimed by their sacrificial lives the liberating and purifying effect of contemplation in a person's life. Titus and Teresa Benedicta rank among many of Carmel's prophets who, for nearly eight centuries, have prophesied that contemplative prayer is a path of self-emptying love that can heal and transform our personal and collective lives.

D.C.

Chapter 4

CHRISTIAN INSIGHT MEDITATION

The inspiration to assimilate Buddhist insight meditation into Carmelite prayer first came in the summer of 1986. Mary Jo Meadow, on leave from Mankato State University, where she was professor of psychology and director of the Religious Studies Program, was devoting the 1985–86 academic year to exploring programs of spiritual practice throughout the United States. For the concluding experience of the year, she had chosen the Carmelite Forum's summer seminar in Carmelite Spirituality, held annually during the last two weeks of June at the Center for Spirituality, St. Mary's College, in Notre Dame, Indiana. At the seminar, Kevin Culligan was lecturing on "The Anthropology of St. John of the Cross" and conducting a workshop on St. John's approach to spiritual direction as revealed in his spiritual classic, *The Dark Night*.

From mid-September to mid-December 1985, Meadow had made a three-month Buddhist *vipassana* retreat at the Insight Meditation Society in Barre, Massachusetts, under the direction of Joseph Goldstein and Sharon Salzberg. After Barre, she visited spiritual centers throughout the United States including the Spiritual Life Institute in Crestone, Colorado, and the Osage Monastery in Sand Springs, Oklahoma. In addition, she did Sufi meditation with Pir Vilayat, studied *A Course in Miracles*, and made the thirty-day Ignatian Spiritual Exercises at a Jesuit retreat house.

Exploring a Hypothesis

By the time she arrived at South Bend in June, Meadow, an experienced meditator for over thirty years, was convinced that the *vipassana* she had practiced at the Insight Meditation Center was highly congruent with the teachings of St. John of the Cross and had much to offer Christian prayer. At the Carmelite seminar, while attending Culligan's lecture and workshop on St. John of the Cross, she was even more deeply struck by the remarkable similarity between Buddhist insight meditation and John of the Cross's presentation of Christian contemplation, especially their common stress on purification and self-emptying as essential ascetical practices.

During the seminar, Meadow asked Culligan's reaction to these impressions. When he affirmed the similarities, the two began to discuss ways in which they might explore them further. At the time, Meadow and Culligan, both licensed clinical psychologists, were active members of the American Psychological Association's Division 36, Psychologists Interested in Religious Issues. In previous years, they had collaborated on presenting symposia and programs in psychology of religion and mysticism at annual APA conventions. They agreed that a logical first step would be to test this insight with their colleagues in an informal Division 36 Conversation Hour at the next APA convention.

Meadow and Culligan entitled their APA presentation: "Similarities between Carmelite Spirituality and Buddhist Meditation: A Psychological Analysis." Culligan presented six areas of similarities between Buddhism and Carmelite Spirituality: both are developmental, produce radical change within individuals, emphasize interiority, have social consequences, demand personal discipline, and involve passive purification. Meadow then described similarities between progress in *vipassana* meditation and the stages of spiritual growth outlined by St. John of the Cross. The psychologists gathered in Division 36's Hospitality Suite responded positively enough to encourage Culligan and Meadow to pursue their insights further.

The international Buddhist-Christian conference was scheduled for August 10–15, 1987, in Berkeley, California, to explore the theme "Buddhism & Christianity: Toward the Human Future." Meadow and Culligan proposed a paper describing the similarities in spiritual development between St. John of the Cross and Theravadan Buddhism, which the program committee accepted. A schedule conflict prevented Culligan from attending the conference, but Meadow read their paper to an audience of about seventy-five interfaith scholars and other persons interested in the spiritual practices of Buddhism and Christianity. Again the response was positive, prompting them to revise their paper and submit it as an article for publication in the *Journal of Transpersonal Psychology*. Their coauthored article, "Congruent Spiritual Paths: Christian Carmelite and Theravadan Buddhist Vipassana," appeared in the 1987 volume of the journal.[1]

Silence and Awareness Retreat

Up to this time, Meadow and Culligan had been publicly comparing Buddhist meditation and Christian prayer only in theory. Meadow, who was continuing intensive practice of insight meditation, also believed that these similarities are true in practice. Specifically, she felt that practicing Theravadan insight meditation leads one toward the emptiness in sense and spirit that John of the Cross maintains is a necessary disposition for union with God. In a retreat with contemplative women in May 1968, Thomas Merton, while discussing a book by Heinrich Dumoulin, a German-Japanese Jesuit, offered a similar opinion that "Zen is nothing but John of the Cross without the Christian theology. As far as the psychological aspect is concerned, that is, the complete emptying of self, it's the same thing and the same approach."[2]

To test Meadow's opinion, Culligan and Meadow began to plan a Christian retreat based on three assumptions. First, although it originates in Theravadan Buddhism, insight meditation itself does not demand belief in the tenets of Buddhist religion. It is essentially a spiritual practice available to all persons of all religions. Second, Christians can use insight meditation as an effective means of deepening their faith and love in Christ Jesus. And third, insight meditation helps Christians embrace fully Jesus' total emptying of self in sense and spirit on the cross, which John of the Cross maintains is the door to the transformation of our lives in God through love.

The retreat itself was to be similar to those offered at the Insight Meditation Society, but within a Christian framework. Meadow and Culligan knew that Christian Zen retreats were offered throughout the United States,[3] but were unaware of any that taught Theravadan insight meditation within a Christian framework, and specifically within the context of the Carmelite spirituality of St. John of the Cross.[4]

With the Carmelite Forum's summer seminar in Carmelite spirituality not scheduled for 1989 and 1990, Culligan and Meadow planned an eight-day retreat in 1989 to be held in Minnesota during the Forum's usual last two weeks of June. They invited Fr. Daniel Chowning, O.C.D., and Fr. Anthony Haglof, O.C.D., two of Culligan's Carmelite confreres with experience in insight meditation, to join them in planning and leading the retreat. In addition to the mailing list for Resources for Ecumenical Spirituality (RES), a non-profit organization founded by Meadow in 1987 to sponsor programs in interfaith spirituality, they announced their retreat to participants in the earlier Carmelite seminars at St. Mary's and to various Carmelite communities of friars, nuns, and laity throughout the United States. They advertised the retreat in periodicals such as *Spiritual Life, Living Prayer, National Catholic Reporter,* and *Sisters Today.*

Finally, on June 25, 1989, sixty-six persons from both coasts as well as from throughout the Midwest and Canada gathered in Minnesota for the first retreat: "Silence and Awareness: A Retreat Experience in Christian-Buddhist Meditation." The following year, from June 29 to July 8, 1990, Meadow and Culligan, assisted by Rebecca Bradshaw, a lay woman experienced in insight meditation, offered the retreat again. In 1991, 1992, and 1993, Culligan, Meadow, and Chowning planned and directed the retreat for thirty to thirty-five participants each year, with Bradshaw's assistance as needed.

From 1989 to 1993, 170 persons made the retreat, some of them several times. To accommodate growing and widespread interest, Resources for Ecumenical Spirituality began in 1994 two additional Silence and Awareness retreats each year in different locations around the United States.

Retreat Goals

In planning these retreats, we (Meadow, Culligan, and Chowning) pursue two goals: to offer a traditionally Christian retreat and to teach the entire insight meditation practice in all its integrity so that retreatants can learn it fully within eight days. Inspiring our planning is the example of men and women from other religious orders — notably the Benedictines and Jesuits — who, in the spirit of the Second Vatican Council, integrate Eastern meditation practices into Christian prayer. We feel strongly that Carmelites, with their long tradition of contemplative prayer, should also respond to this challenge.

We also believe that we are involved in an ancient process in which the Christian faith community takes from the cultures in which it lives those human achievements that help to deepen the understanding and practice of its Christian faith. In the thirteenth century, St. Thomas drew upon the revival of Aristotelian philosophy to more deeply understand Christian beliefs. In our own twentieth century, the Church has enhanced its pastoral care with new understandings of person and community from contemporary psychology and sociology.

Similarly, we are convinced that meditation practices developed over many centuries in the East can enrich Christian life, especially contemplative prayer. With the world now a global village, we no longer need to travel to India or Burma to learn these practices. They are available now throughout the United States and will become increasingly so in the future as our country becomes more pluralistic and multicultural.

On these premises, we plan retreats that include Eucharist, the Sacrament of Reconciliation, and conferences explaining the relationship of insight meditation practice to the deepening of Christian faith, hope, and love, the central challenge in Christian spirituality according to John of the Cross. Within this Christian context, the entire insight meditation practice, both sitting and walking, is taught in a classical, unadulterated manner. The focus is primarily upon learning the practice; no attempt is made in the actual teaching of the practice to demonstrate its relationship with Christian faith. These connections are made in the daily conferences and by the retreatants themselves in the times scheduled for questions of theory and integration.

Retreat Schedule

The daily retreat schedule, based on the *vipassana* retreats at Insight Meditation Society in Barre, Massachusetts, is as follows:.

6:30 A.M.	rising
7:00 A.M.	Eucharist
7:45 A.M.	breakfast
8:45 A.M.	sitting meditation and instruction
10:00 A.M.	walking meditation
11:00 A.M.	sitting meditation
11:45 A.M.	walking meditation or integration questions and answers

12:30 P.M.	lunch optional walking meditation
2:15 P.M.	sitting meditation
3:00 P.M.	walking meditation
3:45 P.M.	sitting meditation and instruction
4:45 P.M.	walking meditation
5:15 P.M.	loving-kindness practice
6:00 P.M.	supper optional walking
7:30 P.M.	retreat conference
8:30 P.M.	walking meditation
9:15 P.M.	sitting meditation
10:00 P.M.	further practice or rest

Silence is maintained throughout the retreat. This excludes eye contact, reading, writing, journaling, and listening to tapes, as well as speech, all of which dissipate meditative energy. However, time is provided each day for either individual or group interviews with retreat team members. These focus on issues in meditation practice, rather than upon personal problem solving, discernment, and decision making.

Retreatants who wish to celebrate the Sacrament of Reconciliation with one of the priests ordinarily do so during individual interview time. Mass is celebrated very quietly. An extended period of silence and a brief homily follow the Gospel reading; the liturgy of the Eucharist emphasizes the liturgical words and gestures and provides another extended period of silence after communion. The Sunday Eucharist, which concludes the retreat, however, is celebrated with song and full active participation.

Breakfasts and lunches are vegetarian, emphasizing whole foods with balanced proteins. The small supper includes a light animal protein. Sugar is used sparingly, as it and heavy foods hinder meditation.

Throughout, the retreat emphasizes interior and exterior silence, concentrated awareness of one's total experiencing, and deepening the spirit of prayer and practice of meditation. The purpose is to help persons become empty of roles, voluntary experiences, and other trappings of ordinary daily life so that they may be more available to God and the purifying love of the Holy Spirit.

Results

Not everyone has found the retreat helpful. Some think there is too little explicit reference to Jesus Christ, too much Buddhist teaching; too little emphasis on Eucharist, Christian prayer, and Carmelite spirituality, too much emphasis on learning the practice of insight meditation; too much of John of the Cross's asceticism, too little of his mysticism. Others believe the retreat leaders should make more explicit effort to integrate the meditation practice into Christian faith. One participant wanted more help from the team to manage the more difficult moments of the retreat when one feels exposed, vulnerable, without masks or defenses; another reported that the retreat's intensity precipitated a three-month clinical depression upon returning home and advised the team to be more careful in screening applicants. These and other reactions we address in more detail in the last section of this book.

Most participants, however, have responded very favorably to the retreat. It is, of course, extremely difficult to measure directly progress in such inner states as purity of heart, emptiness of self, and openness for God, the stated goals of the retreat. But individual persons report that the retreat has brought such benefits as a deepened self-awareness, mindfulness, inner stillness, and interior peace; more discipline in prayer; a stronger desire for God alone; a realization of the need for purification to grow spiritually; reassurance of the compatibility of Buddhist meditation with Christian prayer; healing of memories and emotions and a tool for managing persistent physical pain more gracefully. Many express gratitude for being given help with prayer that they have found nowhere else. Many have adopted insight meditation as their principal form of Christian contemplative prayer.

Christian Insight Meditation

After five years experience with the Silence and Awareness retreat, we conclude that *vipassana,* the meditation practice of Theravadan Buddhism, contributes positively to Christian contemplative life. We name our teaching of this practice within the context of John of the Cross's spirituality "Christian insight meditation." This title avoids the awkwardness most Americans find in pronouncing the Pali word *vipassana;* it also distinguishes the practice from other current approaches to contemplative practice such as Christian Zen, Christian meditation, and centering prayer. Assisted by retreatants' evaluations, we work to improve the theory and practice of Christian insight meditation, believing it helps people to grow in the purity of heart, poverty of spirit, and emptiness of self that dispose them for God's work in their lives. We shall now describe in detail the practice of Christian insight meditation so that you can begin to experience it for yourself.

K.C.

Part II

Meditation
Instructions

Chapter 5

PREPARING FOR INSIGHT PRACTICE

General Directives

The basic insight practice is quite simple, developing concentration and mindful awareness at the same time. We work with a primary object, usually the breath, to establish concentration. We also attend to all other experiences with mindfulness, according to a simple method.

The basic practice consists of four points:

1. Become aware of the "dominant" event occurring in the whole body-mind process.

2. Acknowledge and anchor this awareness by "naming" the process at the very first awareness of it. Make a soft little whisper in the mind called "mental noting."

3. Observe, resting full attention in it, all that happens within the process until it ends.

4. Maintain a soft, gentle, persistent willingness. Do not try to make any experience come, stay, or be a particular way; do not try to prevent or push away any experience.

The following chapters give explicit instructions for how to work with different types of experience. Learning insight practice is simplest when you take time to consolidate working with each aspect of it before going on to the next. We recommend that you spend some time working with each instruction before adding others.

Establishing Posture

Insight practice is usually done sitting in a firm and unmoving posture. You may sit in a straight chair or cross-legged on a *zafu* (round sitting cushion) or other firm cushion on the floor, or kneel on a *seiza* (sitting) or prayer bench. Putting a mat or folded blanket underneath you cushions legs and knees. Initially, while still establishing basic concentration, you may move to adjust an uncomfortable posture. Eventually you should sit as still as possible.

Sitting in a good posture, with a relatively straight spine, helps prevent stress on muscles. Holding the back straight is easiest when the hip bones are higher than the knee bones. If using a cushion, sit near the front edge so that all the buttocks, but none of the upper legs, are on the cushion. The simplest cross-legged posture is called Burmese style. Bend the knee of one leg and draw the heel in as close to the groin as you can. Bend the other knee, and pull that leg in as close to the first one as possible. Both knees should rest on the floor. You can help leg muscles loosen up by practicing sitting outside of formal meditation time. While watching television or talking with friends or family, simply sit cross-legged on your cushion.

Sitting benches throw the back into a good alignment, but ankles often are stiff at the beginning. This discomfort will lessen in time. If you meditate sitting in a chair, do not lean against the back. A chair that slopes slightly toward the front is most helpful. Putting one-half to one-inch blocks under the back legs of a chair or obtaining a firm foam wedge for the seat of the chair helps produce this slope. Both feet should rest firmly on the ground, one to two feet apart.

The shoulders should be over the hip bones and the earlobes in line with the shoulders. It helps to tuck the chin slightly and have the back of the top of the head as the highest body point. Once seated, you can align the body and adjust the curve in the spine by pulling the navel forward or pushing it back. Check to be sure that the shoulders are hanging loosely and are not hunched up around the neck. Place your hands however it feels comfortable to rest them without wanting to move them.

When correctly placed, the bones will simply stack themselves on top of each other. You can then hold an erect posture with no strain or effort. Until posture is well established, check at the beginning of each sitting to be sure that you are not tightly holding the body in place and that the shoulders hang loosely. Do not expect to have perfect posture immediately. You may play around with posture until it feels right. Erect posture is important, not for any "magical" reasons, but because it helps to minimize strain on the body.

Protecting the Practice

Protecting the practice means keeping ourselves motivated to work at it. There are some time-honored ways to protect practice. You might reflect on the beauty of a saintly life or on the merits of a religious figure you admire. You might offer a short prayer of some kind or remind yourself of the high goal of spiritual practice. You might do loving-kindness practice, which is explained in chapter 11. If you work best with negative images, you might reflect on the shortness of life or the ugliness of a disordered heart.

One special protection is an act of surrender. This expresses our willingness to be with all meditation experiences as a healing offered us. Surrender opens us to accept the needed purgation that practice effects in us. It helps maintain a soft gentleness that does not grasp after or push away any experience.

Many Buddhists begin meditation practice with "May I be surrendered to the *Dhamma*." *Dhamma* is a very rich word with many meanings — including the way, the path, Truth, Reality, realities, the practice, that which supports and upholds us and the pattern of all that is. Similarities to Christian understandings of both the *Logos* (Word) and the Holy Spirit are obvious. You may want to begin your sittings with an act of surrender to the healing and sanctifying power of the Holy Spirit.

M.J.M.

Chapter 6

WORKING WITH
THE PRIMARY OBJECT

Choosing the Primary Object

To begin meditation practice, we choose a primary object, a basic experience to use as "home base." As many practices do, we usually use the breath since it is almost always present. (As concentration deepens, the breath may temporarily cease.) Going back to the breath at regular intervals deepens concentration as a foundation for awareness practice. It also gives us a focus for attention when there are no other experiences to watch.

It is easiest to start where you experience the breath most clearly. Sitting with your eyes closed, pay attention to the flow of the breath. Try to discern in which of three places you feel the sensations of breathing most clearly. Do not have any preconceived ideas about where it is best to feel the breath. Check where the upper lip meets the nostrils, the rising and falling of the chest, and the rising and falling of the diaphragm or belly. If no one place stands out more clearly than the others, see if the mind more comfortably gravitates to one place. Any of the three places will do. If one place stands out, choose it as the primary object. If none does, arbitrarily choose any one of the three. Once you have chosen a place, you should use it regularly unless a teacher tells you to change it, although occasionally you may work with breath at a different place.

Beginning the Practice

If you have used breath awareness in any other form of meditation practice, please set that aside. The way we work with the breath in this practice prepares us for the rest of awareness practice. Other ways of working with the breath will compete with mindfulness practice, and you will not really be doing either properly.

Sitting in a comfortably erect posture, become aware of the place you have chosen to watch the breath. Hold awareness there without moving it around and feel all of the sensations of the breath at that place. As soon as you notice that an inhalation is starting, softly note "in" by silently whispering the word in your mind. If you are watching at the chest or diaphragm, you may note "rising" if you prefer. Put all your awareness in the sensations of the breath at the place where you are watching until the inhalation ends.

When you become aware that an exhalation is starting, softly note "out" or "falling." Put all your awareness in the sensations of the breath at the place where you are watching until the exhalation ends. Continue in this way to experience inhalations and exhalations of the breath. Try to note the very beginning of each inhalation and exhalation. However, do not anticipate the start of the breath; that would make the note a command to the body to breathe.

Make the mental note loud enough to help hold you on target, but not so loud as to draw attention away from the sensations. Remember that the note should be a very soft whisper in the mind, usually using no more than 5 percent of available mental energy. You may make a very short note at the beginning of the breath, stretch it out across the whole breath, or choose something in between. Do whatever most helps you stay focused.

Be in very close touch with all the sensations of the breath at the place you are observing. Do not "look down at" the sensations from above or at an image of them. Put your awareness "inside" the sensations themselves. Make no attempt to control the breath in any way; let it flow just as it does by itself. Smooth, bumpy, long, short, even, irregular — all are okay.

When the Breath Is Not There

When you become aware that attention has wandered from the breath, acknowledge the experience to which you are attending by softly noting it with a descriptive word — thinking, hearing, and so on. Then gently bring awareness back to the breath. Getting lost in thought is the most common early experience; it says nothing about your ability to do this practice. So long as you return to the breath as soon as you become aware of wandering, you are doing the practice correctly.

If discomfort keeps drawing awareness from the breath, first try noting it and returning to the breath. If you still feel need, you may gently adjust posture to reduce it. Also note any other sensation or emotion that draws awareness, and then return to the breath. Eventually all these other experiences will not be treated as wandering from the task; they become part of the practice after you have learned how to work with them.

If there is a pause between breaths, move awareness to feeling the whole body sitting. Note "sitting" and feel the body until the next breath starts. If the pause is long, add awareness of a place where part of the body is touching. This may be buttocks on seat, hand on leg, or any other place you can feel a touch sensation. Note "touching" and feel its sensations. If the pause is very long, go back and forth between "sitting" and "touching" until the breath starts again. Do not try to make pauses in the breath occur.

Some General Instructions

Sometimes working with the breath is very difficult, such as when you have a head cold. You may then use sitting-

touching as the primary object, holding awareness on each
for about the length of a breath.

To begin practice well, you need to build some concentration and become comfortable working with breath awareness
before adding other steps. Spend at least half a dozen hours
working just with the breath before going on to the next
instruction.

M.J.M.

Chapter 7

WORKING WITH BODY SENSATIONS

Buddhist psychology recognizes six senses: mind, seeing, hearing, smelling, tasting, and body sensations. This chapter will teach you how to work with body experiences. Body sensations fall into three main types: temperature changes, feelings of movement, and touch sensations. We work with all of them similarly.

Working with Awareness of Temperature

When we meditate, often we become aware that the body feels cooler or warmer. Sometimes a particular part of the body feels like it is burning or freezing. When such awareness stays on the fringe of attention, we remain centered on the breath.

However, if awareness of temperature draws attention from the breath, immediately focus full awareness on that sensation. Note it with a descriptive word, such as "coolness," "burning," "warm," or "freezing." Do not try to hold on to breath awareness; instead, put all the awareness inside the feeling of temperature.

If the experience ends, or if attention wanders to something else, go back to the breath. If the awareness of temperature continues, repeat the note about every five or ten seconds — often enough to hold attention firmly, but not so often as to distract you from feeling the temperature sensation. After several minutes, go back to the breath. If the same awareness again draws attention, work with it again for several minutes. So long as it keeps drawing attention, you can work with it. Remember, though, to take your "breathers" back to the breath.

Working with Movement Sensations

Sometimes the body will feel like it is moving. When such sensation is strong enough to draw attention away from the breath, sink awareness into that experience. Immediately note it with an appropriate word, such as "floating," "swaying," "vibrating," or "bouncing." Let go of the breath, and put full attention inside the movement sensation. Do not check to see if the body actually is moving. If you experience moving, it is "real" for the practice and you work with it.

Repeat the noting as explained above for temperature changes. Also follow those instructions on returning to the breath. When working with movement, add the intention to still the body when returning to the breath. Otherwise, if actual movement is occurring, it will almost certainly again claim attention. We want to leave room for another experience to surface. However, work with movement whenever it draws your attention.

Working with Touch Sensations

Touch sensations can be of many kinds. In initial practice, most of them are unpleasant. We are so accustomed to tuning out body sensations, or making minor adjustments in posture to eliminate them, that we do not really know how the body feels most of the time. When we sit in mindful attention, these discomforts start coming into awareness. This initial unpleasantness will lessen.

When a body sensation becomes strong enough to draw attention from the breath, work with it. As soon as you become aware that attention has moved to it, sink awareness into the experience, letting go of breath awareness, and note it with an appropriate word describing the sensation. Some examples are "itching," "cramping," and "tingling." You can use generic words like "sensing" or "touching" if a more descriptive word does not easily come to mind. Follow the instructions above on repeating the note and on returning to the breath.

If a touch sensation is particularly intense, you may return to the breath more frequently to rest the mind. You can also place the sensation along the edges of awareness for a while and deliberately focus attention on the breath. Sometimes making the area of sensation being watched either larger or smaller makes it easier to stay with the sensation.

Some Other Considerations

Once we start work with body sensations, we try to sit as still as possible so that we do not cut off experiences as soon as they arise. Do not move on the first impulse; see if you are willing to settle back and be with the experience a little longer. However, this practice is to be done very gently. Do not overcontrol, tense up, or otherwise fight an experience. When you reach the end of willingness, make whatever adjustment is needed, go back to the breath, and begin again. Willingness will gradually grow. You will also notice that petty environmental discomforts bother you less.

Gerunds, words that end in "ing," are often the best words to use as notes because they capture the sense of an ongoing process. However, do not look hard for just the right word to note meditation experiences. Over time, a vocabulary will automatically build to note different kinds of experiences.

Awareness practice with body sensations can help heal a wide range of psychosomatic problems. It seems also to release old traumas to the body and has occasionally healed serious medical illness. You should not expect dramatic healing, though, as this is relatively rare.

Work with body sensations for at least half a dozen hours of practice before adding another instruction. This will give you a solid grounding in doing the practice.

M.J.M.

Chapter 8

WORKING WITH THE OTHER SENSES AND THINKING

This chapter teaches you learn how to work with the other four body senses. It also gives instructions on working with thinking, to begin work on the mind.

Working with the Other Senses

In awareness practice, we note and attend to our own experiences only. When the body is cramping, tingling, or itching, we can properly say that this is our experience. However, the different kinds of seeing, hearing, smelling, and tasting we experience are only simple experiences of these senses. The bird is chirping, the car is roaring, and so on. These are not your experiences; you are just hearing.

This makes work with the other four senses — seeing, hearing, smelling, and tasting — easy compared to body sensations. We have only one way of noting each of them: "seeing," "hearing," "smelling," or "tasting." Use the guidelines given for body sensations for attending to these experiences, noting them, and going back to the breath.

Sometimes we have repetitious experiences. Someone may be running a lawn mower, and the mind keeps going to the sound. Or the same kind of visual imagery may occur repetitively. In such instances, note and work with the experience the first few times it draws attention. Then try to place it along the edges of awareness and stay on the breath to allow other experiences to surface. However, if it draws you strongly, work with it again.

Some people get a lot of visual imagery as soon as they close their eyes to meditate. Others are flooded with sound. Still other people may practice for years and seldom experience such things. There is no right or wrong way. Work with the practice as it happens for you. Do not ask if what you see, hear, smell, or taste is "real." If you experience it, it is "real" for the practice. Do not worry about whether the mind is creating experiences or not. It does this every night when you dream. Meditation is just one other situation that can cause this to happen.

Thought and Escaping the Present Moment

Thinking is a most peculiar activity. With thought, we create alternative worlds to live in, in place of the actual reality of moment-to-moment experience. When thoughts come, we often get seduced by them and want to continue living in this world we are creating. When this happens, we are no longer meditating.

We escape from the present moment into thought in three basic ways. First, we may cling to the past. When we get caught up in memories or replay past experiences, we are doing this. We cannot experience the past directly; it is not happening now. When we try to hold on to it, we re-create it in the world of mind.

Sometimes we try to make the future present — again, an impossible endeavor. We can only create thoughts about the future, and then live in this unreal world we are making. We do that when we get caught up in planning, rehearsing, or anticipating.

Sometimes we simply just push away the present moment or distance ourselves from it. We may judge experiences or ourselves, complain mentally about what is happening or stage a drama with self as the star. At other times, we may analyze what is happening or keep a running commentary going in the mind. We sometimes create an entirely imaginary fantasy world to inhabit when we make up stories about what is happening.

There is nothing wrong with thoughts coming. Thought is perfectly natural, and we could not stop it if we tried. We even want to see the thoughts that come, as some insights and other important information can come in the form of thought. However, we do not want to get lost in thought since that closes down meditation. It stops the very process that brings up important understandings.

Working with Thinking

Every meditator spends time lost in thought. Sometimes we can see thoughts come and go without following off after them, but at the beginning we are more likely to get lost in them. Do not be concerned about this; it will improve with practice. Just persistently note "thinking" as soon as you become aware of it, and then return to the breath. A major problem is that sometimes we don't want to note thought and leave it. You must be careful not to let greed for thoughts draw you away from meditation practice.

You may have noticed that sensations can continue while you focus mindful awareness on them. Thinking is different; to keep a train of thought going, we usually must get lost in it. Once we turn the bright spotlight of awareness onto thinking, it evaporates like mist.

You should immediately return to the breath after noting thinking; remember, the thought will die when awareness is focused on it. It may take a little while before you clearly see this. If you wait to see what will happen instead of returning to the breath when you become aware of thought, another thought will come quickly. Pretty soon you will be lost in thinking again.

We refine work with thought by noting the kind of thinking we do. This is not noting the content of thought, the story line of the thoughts, but just the type of thought. So you might use such notes as "remembering," "planning," "self-dramatizing," "complaining," and so on. This helps us see where we spend most of our time running away — into the past or future, or just pushing away the present. We realize this without thinking about it; it comes from just doing the noting.

A Suggestion

Trying to add too much all at once can be confusing. You may find it helpful to work with either thought or the other senses for a while before adding the other object. If you first work long enough with one, adding the other should then be easier. You may also want to get used to just noting "thinking" for a while before trying to note the type of thought. Be sure you have worked with all sensations and thought for at least half a dozen hours before going on to the next instruction.

M.J.M.

Chapter 9

WORKING WITH MIND-STATES

Understanding Mind-States

To understand easily what a mind-state is, think of it as a dye or tint in the mind. This coloring of the mind affects everything else we experience. A mind-state is like a pair of colored glasses we wear. Everything is seen through it.

Mind-states include emotions, states of awareness, sets, and moods. We are most easily aware of strong mind-states like anger, sleepiness, fear, or joy. When you are angry, anger colors everything you experience. When intense joy is present, even difficult circumstances or events are not seen as a problem because they are colored by the joy. Sleepiness puts a haze and heaviness on everything.

In conditioned reality (explained in chapter 2), mind-states are always present. Some are very subtle, and attention is not likely to be drawn to them. At the end of a very peaceful day, you might realize that the whole day was colored by this state of peacefulness. Usually you won't be aware of this unless you stop to reflect on it.

All mind-states have associated body-states. Some of these are obvious. Sadness brings tightening and heaviness in the chest and choking in the throat. If you are about to cry, you feel stinging in the eyes. When you actually do cry, there are heaving, shaking, and sobbing movements. With sleepiness, we have heaviness in the eyelids and sinking feelings. Anger often brings heat and tense muscles. The body-states connected to very subtle mind-states may be difficult to feel.

Mind-States and Emotional Healing

Insight meditation practice can heal much of our unfinished emotional business that has intense mind-states associated with it. However, we must do something different from how we handle emotions in our everyday lives, which has not worked well. We usually do one of two unhelpful things with our strong emotions.

Sometimes, when we feel one coming, we do everything we can to avoid it. We call a friend to talk on the phone, escape into watching whatever happens to be on television, go out looking for something to do — or reach for our addiction! We can hold off the bad feeling for a while. But two hours, or two days, or two weeks later, it comes back again. We have not solved anything. We have not dealt with it.

A second mistake is the opposite of the first one. We get completely lost and "drown" in the mind-state. We lose all perspective and start feeding the mind-state with thoughts that intensify it. We may grind around on resentments, calling to mind all the shoddy things that someone did to us. We may think of all the things that could go wrong tomorrow when we interview for that job we really want, and get lost in anxiety. We may feed sadness with self-pity or melodrama, talking to ourselves about all our woes or sorrows. Some people go on crying jags, trying to "cry it all out."

It can be terribly tempting to think that, if we just really get into such mind-states, we can resolve them. Instead, though, this simply strengthens the mind-state. The more we ruminate on a hurt feeling, for example, the more deeply it ingrains itself in the mind. We give it a tighter hold on us.

When we work with mind-states in awareness practice, we fully experience them, not pushing them away. But we also do not get lost in our emotions or feed them with thinking. We avoid both these errors that do not work well for us in our ordinary everyday experience with mind-states. This meditative way of experiencing them allows them to be healed.

How to Work with Mind-States

When a mind-state draws attention from the primary object, let go of the breath and fully sink awareness into the mind-state. As soon as you notice the mind-state, also note it with an appropriate word such as "sadness," "sleepiness," "anger," "fear," and so on.

Do not go looking through the body for bodily experiences that go with the mind-state. Do sit with openness, though, to be aware of what is happening in the body. If a body experience comes into awareness, note it with an appropriately descriptive word. Treat it like all other body experiences.

You must be very alert to catch thought when working with mind-states. As soon as a thought comes, see it clearly, note the thinking, and return immediately to the breath. Thinking thoughts associated with a mind-state invites it to stay around and grow stronger. You do not want to chase the mind-state away, but you also do not want to do anything to encourage it to stay or intensify.

You can go back and forth between noting the mental and bodily sides of a mind-state, as different experiences related to it occur. You should be noting something at least every five to ten seconds. So long as we are noting, we are not lost in the experience. We are both experiencing and observing at the same time.

After working with the mind-state for a few minutes, take a breather back to the breath. If another experience draws attention to itself, work with it. If the same mind-state draws you again, stay with it. You can spend most of the sitting on the same mind-state if it keeps calling you to it, but remember to take breaks to the breath. This keeps concentration strong and makes space for other experiences to draw the awareness.

Build your awareness practice carefully. Work with mind-states added to your practice for at least half a dozen hours before adding the next instruction.

M.J.M.

Chapter 10

WORKING WITH
THE POINTS OF FREEDOM

Feeling-tone and intention are two special mind-states. They are very important in insight meditation practice because they are points of freedom. Careful attentiveness to feeling-tone helps prevent mental impurity, keeps us from getting lost in unwholesome mind-states. Working with intention stems behavioral impurity; it gives us space to be able to say "no" to unhelpful choices.

Understanding the Chain of Behavior

Everything we experience has a feeling-tone — a degree of pleasantness, unpleasantness, or neutrality. Ordinarily, we are not aware of this until it precipitates us into some re-action to it. Pleasantness, or anticipating pleasantness, draws out greed — such as lust, avarice, gluttony, and so on. Unpleasantness, or anticipating unpleasantness, draws out aversion — such as anger, sadness, fear, anxiety, and so on. When feeling-tone is neutral, the experience does not grip us strongly and we "space out"; we become inattentive, bored, or sleepy. This puts us in delusion, ignorance of the true nature of what is happening. Paying careful attention to feeling-tone shows us that these conditioned emotional reactions can be a choice. We can become free of the unwholesome mind-states that so often keep us in mental turmoil.

An intention forms before every action we take. Sometimes we are clearly aware of it as an intention, but sometimes it feels only like some impulse or urge arising in us. Once an intention becomes strong enough, action follows automatically; we are past being able to decide about it. When we become clearly aware of intentions, we can change our mind about them by countering them with a contrary intention before they propel us into action. This helps free us from committing wrong actions.

For all of our behavior, we can trace five important parts. First, there is an experience. Second is its feeling-tone, which comes simultaneously with the experience. Then comes reactivity to it, the mind-states arising from the pleasantness, unpleasantness, or neutrality of feeling-tone. When the mind-state becomes sufficiently intense, it gives rise to an intention to act upon the greed, aversion, or delusion that has arisen. When an intention becomes strong enough, it propels us into action, the final step. So, we have EXPERIENCE → FEELING-TONE → REACTIVE MIND-STATES → INTENTIONS → OVERT BEHAVIOR. The points of freedom are between feeling-tone and reactive mind-states, and between intentions and overt behavior.

Each of these five steps is, in itself, another experience that triggers its own chain. So, our actual behavior in everyday life is a complex network of many simultaneous chains from experience to action. Meditation practice slows our experience down enough so that we can actually see all these parts. Working with them in practice then carries over to everyday life.

How to Work with Feeling-Tone

We work with feeling-tone like any other mind-state. Do not search through your mind looking for it, but sit with an openness to be aware of it. At times, it will arise in the mind as a dominant experience. Intensely pleasant or unpleasant feeling-tone is the easiest to see; neutrality is usually not seen until practice is rather advanced.

When feeling-tone draws the attention, sink full awareness into its quality of pleasantness, unpleasantness, or neutrality. Note it simply as "pleasant," "unpleasant," or "neutral." If associated body experiences come into awareness, work with them also. When you are experiencing a lot of greed or aversion, becoming aware of feeling-tone is very helpful. This also assists work with intense sensations. Eventually you will see that mind-state reactions are voluntary and also that even intense feeling-tone will finally dim and change without your doing anything.

Awareness of feeling-tone is helpful in everyday life, too. When emotions come up, try to see to which pleasantness or unpleasantness you are reacting. You should be able to see that the problem is not really that unpleasant other person or this delicious ice cream, but simply that you are reacting to feeling-tone. This awareness will greatly moderate unhelpful reactions to life events.

How to Work with Intention

When you feel an impulse to move while meditating, be aware that this is an intention and note it as "intending." Careful noting of intention often helps us counter it with a contrary intention so we can sit unmoving. Watching intention also shows us that, without our doing anything at all about it, intentions will eventually go away. This teaches us that all urges will end whether we act on them or not.

If you make a voluntary movement, be sure to note the arising intention. Also note the actions of scratching, lifting, turning — whatever the movement — while paying attention to the sensations you feel while moving.

Becoming aware of intentions in daily life is very helpful. Whenever you react strongly to any experience, intentions are apt to arise. By being prepared for them, you can accept them without being drawn into unthinking action.

The Final Steps

Work with feeling-tone and intention ends the basic instructions for formal sitting practice. The next chapter explains some other practices commonly done along with awareness sitting practice.

M.J.M.

Chapter 11

WORKING WITH AUXILIARY PRACTICES
Walking and Loving-Kindness Practices, Sharing Merit

Walking Practice

To do formal walking practice, choose a path ten to twenty steps in length. You will walk back and forth along this path. By just going back and forth, we pretty quickly realize we are not going anywhere and settle down to pay attention simply to the walking itself. Hold the hands however you wish, but do not keep changing them around, as that distracts you. Cast your eyes on the ground about two to four feet ahead; do not look around.

Divide the walking period into three parts at different walking speeds. At the beginning, take about one-third of the walking period for each part. Later you will see that sometimes you need more of the brisk movement for energy, and at other times walking quite slowly for most of the period feels appropriate.

First, walk at near normal pace. As you walk, note either "step, step" or else "left, right." Pay attention to the sensations in the moving leg. If all you can feel is the pressure of putting the foot down, that is okay. Do not actually look at the leg, but sink awareness into feeling the sensations.

When you reach the end of the path, stop. Note "standing" and feel the whole body standing. Closing the eyes briefly and/or running attention up or down the body some- times helps. Then turn around. As soon as you start the turn, note "turning" and feel the movement of the body turning. Then go back over the path noting each step and feeling the sensations in the moving leg.

For the second part, go more slowly. For each step, note both "lifting" and "placing." Try to feel how the sensations of lifting are different from those of placing. Keep attention on the sensations in the moving leg. Each time you reach the end of the path, note "standing" and "turning" as described above.

For the third part of walking practice, you may go as slowly as you can while still maintaining balance. Note four parts to each step: "lifting," "moving," "placing," and "shifting." After shifting weight, bring attention to the back leg and begin another step. This walking will look peculiar, since it is not how we ordinarily walk. Both feet will be flat on the floor during the shifting. You should fully complete one step before beginning the next. If you have trouble with balance, taking smaller steps will help. Stand and turn at the end of the path as described above.

If attention goes to other things while walking, try to make them "background" awareness and hold the attention on sensations in the moving leg. Do not note other things while walking. If they keep drawing attention, stop walking to note and attend to them briefly. Then bring attention back to the leg, and again begin walking.

If you want to refine walking practice, add working with intention. You can observe and note the intention before turning and before beginning to walk each length. During very slow walking, you may want to note the intention before each lifting movement. Do not note intentions in the middle parts of a step.

During retreats, walking practice is very important to bal- ance energy. With the sitting practice, it makes a complete meditation practice. Off retreat, we are usually energized by other activities, but some people still find walking very helpful. When the mind is especially scattered, some walking practice before sitting may gather it in, so that you are really centered when you sit. Some people also like to do walking practice just for its own sake. Outside of formal practice, awareness of walking while moving around during the day helps keeps us centered and mindful.

Loving-Kindness (*Metta*) Practice

Loving-kindness (*metta*, in the Pali language of early Buddhist writings) practice consists of calling down blessings on ourselves and others.[1] It may be offered for any being you can image, including animals. You need not image them, but should have some sense of the being to whom you are sending *metta* while practicing.

To do *metta*, take a comfortable posture. You may sit, stand, walk, or lie down. Unless walking, it usually helps to close the eyes. Whenever you become uncomfortable, change your posture. You may take a few intentionally deep breaths to relax. Some people find it helpful to focus attention on the heart.

Many people begin *metta* practice with forgiveness, saying something like this. "I ask forgiveness of all beings whom I have hurt or harmed in any way. I freely forgive all beings who have hurt or harmed me in any way. I freely forgive myself."

Next take a few minutes to recall things about yourself that you can celebrate. We ponder helpful choices we have made to stir up feelings of gentle caring for ourselves. The awareness practice shows what is wrong with us, but that is only half the story. We need also to know what is right about ourselves. We must feel loving-kindness toward ourselves to feel it toward any other being. If you can think of nothing else, be pleased that you have chosen to learn to meditate.

When you work with any other beings, take a minute to recall some of their positive characteristics. You may image them in your heart or in front of you and speak as if directly to them, "May you...." You need not actually image them if you do not image easily, but simply hold some sense of them.

You may use any blessings you choose. Usually four or five is a helpful number. Repeat each benediction as many times as you wish before moving onto the next one, or simply keep going through your set of phrases over and over again. However, be sure to keep repeating the phrases; do not let your mind simply go empty. Use the same blessings for everyone blessed during any one sitting of *metta*. At other sittings you may choose different blessings.

Always begin with yourself and end with "all beings everywhere." Those to whom you send *metta* in the middle may vary. You may move outward geographically — such as from yourself to all in the room with you, all in the city, the state, the country, the hemisphere, on earth. You may move out by emotional distance to benefactors (including parents), other family members, friends, colleagues, clients or students, acquaintances, people you don't know but see at times, and so on. To work with a problem relationship, go from yourself to a benefactor, a friend, a neutral person (someone you do not know well enough to have feelings about), and then the problem person. Some people like to go through lists of friends, including pets, and/or relatives in the middle part of *metta* practice.

Here is a set of traditional blessings:

May I (you, all beings everywhere) be safe from inner and outer danger.

May I (you, all beings everywhere) be happy and peaceful in mind.

May I (you, all beings everywhere) be strong and healthy in body.

May I (you, all beings everywhere) take care of myself (yourself, themselves) with happy ease.

May I (you, all beings everywhere) come to union with God.

Metta is not a part of awareness practice but is a form of concentrative meditation. Some people do normal-length sittings of *metta* regularly or occasionally. Others use it to help their awareness practice. Doing some *metta* "softens" the mind and makes practice more gentle. A few minutes of *metta* at the start of a sitting helps "protect" the practice by keeping us motivated. *Metta* can also be practiced in daily life; we can send it to others whenever we are inclined to do so.

Sharing Merit

Merit is whatever makes us "shine within." All acts of virtue — piety, goodness, spiritual practice, and the like — create merit. We can share it with any other being, living or dead. Some people share merit after each meditation sitting. Sharing merit is, itself, a meritorious action and is said to increase merit. So the more we try to bankrupt ourselves for others, the richer in merit we become. This is not an ideal motive, however!

If you want to share merit, you may use a simple formula like this. "May the fruits of my (generosity, virtue, spiritual practice) be for the good of (my mother, Jane Doe, all beings everywhere)." Simply name the meritorious action and the person(s) with whom you wish to share. You may also go through a litany, repeating the phrase a number of times naming a different meritorious action each time. The merit can be shared with the same or different people.

M.J.M.

Part III

Three Levels of Purification

St. John of the Cross and Theravadan Buddhism Compared

Now that you have started practicing insight meditation, we offer a theoretical context for integrating this practice into Christian spirituality. We compare St. John of the Cross with Theravadan Buddhism at three different levels of purification. Both traditions hold that spiritual seekers must traverse these levels in their journey to union with the Absolute. At each level, we present in separate chapters the teachings of both John of the Cross and the Buddha. A brief summary chapter then integrates the two traditions within Jesus' call to purity of heart and shows the implications of this level for the practice of Christian insight meditation.

Section One

The First Level of Purification

CONDUCT

Chapter 12

ST. JOHN OF THE CROSS
Purification of Disordered Appetites

"Cleanness of heart," writes John of the Cross, commenting on the beatitude Jesus proclaimed, "is nothing less than the love and grace of God." Jesus calls the pure of heart blessed because "they are taken with love, for blessedness is derived from nothing else but love" (N2, 12, 1).

Love and Grace:
The Christian Path of Purification

Christian love is our response to God who has first loved us unconditionally in the life, death, and resurrection of Jesus Christ. In practice, it demands continual conversion of mind and heart to imitate Jesus in all our actions. It requires interior emptying of our spirit through faith to allow Jesus to awaken within us. It means openness to receive God's gracious self-communication that ultimately heals our sinfulness, transforms us in Jesus, and establishes us finally in the eternal blessedness of the Trinity.

The path of Christian purification demands conversion of life, interior emptying, and openness to God's revelation. This parallels the three Buddhist levels of purification — conduct, mental contents, and the heart — leading to *nibbana*, the only unconditioned and unchanging reality. Motivated by Christian faith and love and enlightened by Buddhist teaching and practice, Christians who embrace the path of purification discover Jesus as they have never known him before. They follow him more faithfully in their daily lives, experience his awakening within their hearts, and are gradually transformed into his life of wisdom and compassion.

Union with God through Love:
Goal of Christian Life

The goal of Christian life is perfect union with God through love. As a spiritual guide, John of the Cross wants to help persons realize this union as quickly as possible. He understands union with God to mean simply a union of our will with God's will. This "union of likeness," begotten in mutual love, exists when "God's will and the soul's are in conformity, so that nothing in the one is repugnant to the other" (A2, 5, 3). Guiding persons to this union quickly consists, not in providing a secret or magic formula, but in pointing out the most direct path possible.

To imagine this union of wills, think of the sun coming through a window. When the window is dirty, distinguishing the sunlight from the window is easy. The smudges on the window reveal clearly that the window and the sun are two separate entities.

However, wash the window perfectly clean and remove all the smudges; then distinguishing the sunlight from the window is virtually impossible. Although they remain separate, the two appear to have become one. If you have ever walked smack into a perfectly cleaned window-door leading to a sun deck, you know from experience that the window seems to have disappeared, leaving only the sunlight.

Using this analogy, John teaches that although we always remain distinct from God, we can be so united with God's will that we appear in all our actions to be God. We become "God by participation" (A2, 5, 7), filled with the light of God's wisdom and the warmth of divine compassion. For this union, we must first be purified of everything that prevents its happening. Like the smudges on the window that must be wiped away before the window "becomes" the sun, so we must be purified of sin and its effects before we can be completely transformed into the life of God.

Levels of Purification

To achieve this union of transformation, we must be purified, John teaches, through mortification, faith, and contemplation. Each purifies a different level of our personality. Mortification purifies "sense," or that area of our life which is centered in sensory experiences as we relate to objects in the visible world around us. Faith purifies "spirit," or that dimension of our life that enables us to know, to love, and to relate to that which transcends the visible universe. Finally, contemplation, God's self-communication to us in knowledge and love, purifies our entire being of everything that prevents our total transformation in God.

This purification is a collaborative work between God and ourselves. We do what we can through mortification and faith to purify sense and spirit; God purifies our entire person through contemplation. We cannot achieve union with God by mortification and faith alone; yet neither does God purify us with divine loving knowledge unless we dispose ourselves in sense and spirit to receive this gift.

These three levels of purification are not consecutive, as though mortification precedes faith, and faith must be perfect before contemplation begins. They occur simultaneously, although at different stages of the journey one form of purification may predominate.

For example, beginners concentrate mostly on mortification, although saying "no" to disordered desires is always part of the spiritual journey, no matter how far advanced we are. Contemplation, God's self-communication, or the "secret and peaceful and loving inflow of God" (N1, 10, 6) into the soul, is the main purification of persons advanced in the spiritual journey. However, it is never absent, even as we begin to walk the spiritual path. And, obviously for Christians, faith, together with hope and love, must be present at every stage of the journey, although these virtues are expressed or experienced differently at different stages along the way.

Purification for union with God is thus a lifelong process. In John's opinion, relatively few are so purified in this life that their wills are completely one with God's, as the perfectly clear window is one with the light of the sun. Nonetheless, it is possible through God's grace and human effort. Mary of Nazareth is a perfect example of one so united, as are other acknowledged saints, like Francis of Assisi and Teresa of Avila, and perhaps millions of others of whom John was unaware.

But regardless of the level of holiness attained in this life, we cannot be totally united with God through love until our purification is complete. If not finished in this world, then it continues hereafter, possibly in the death process itself or in the vision of the Risen Jesus. No matter how and when it happens, we will not be completely united with and transformed in God until our hearts are purified through mortification, faith, and contemplation.

We shall now describe each level of purification in more detail. We begin with the senses and the mortification of disordered appetites.

Disordered Appetites:
Obstacle to Divine Union

What today we call desire, John called appetite. Appetite or desire is needed for human survival, growth, and development. Appetite moves us to unite with objects that promote human life. We would probably not eat unless we had an appetite for food and enjoyed the pleasure it gives us; the human race would likely end if men and women stopped desiring one another and the physical pleasure their union causes.

Every desire for union with an object is implicitly a desire for union with God, the Ultimate Fulfillment of both the individual person and the entire human family. And it is through a lifetime of ordered relationships with objects — persons, places, things, ideas, memories — that we come finally to union with God.

History demonstrates, however, that many do not seek their personal fulfillment in God, but instead choose objects of desire as their ultimate goal in life. They habitually choose to satisfy themselves completely with the pleasure objects give them, or money, or power, or reputation, or countless other things. When this happens, a person's appetites have become disordered. They are no longer ordered to union with God. Until these disordered appetites are purified, union with God through love is impossible.

Jesus said: "People cannot serve two masters: they will either hate the one and love the other, or they will be devoted to the one and despise the other. You cannot serve both God and money" (Mt 6:24). In this same vein, John of the Cross reasons that "two contraries cannot coexist in the same subject" (A1, 4, 2). Disordered desires for created things drive the Spirit of God from the soul; we cannot have both God and creatures as the ultimate end of our longings and desires. He explains: "A person has only one will, and if that is encumbered or occupied by anything, the person will not possess the freedom, solitude, and purity requisite for divine transformation" (A1, 11, 6).

Not only do disordered appetites preclude union with God through love, they also damage our personality. Every choice we make affects us. Just as acts of virtue bring us mildness, peace, comfort, light, purity, and strength, so acting out disordered desires torments, fatigues, wearies, blinds, and weakens us (A1, 12, 5). As a result, *we* become disordered and dysfunctional.

We can observe this in our own behavior when we are driven by desire for something, even something as insignificant as a cigarette. The desire quickly takes control of us, enslaves us to a rounded piece of paper three inches long packed with tobacco, and leaves us no peace until it is satisfied. Appetites "resemble little children, restless and hard to please, always whining to their mother for this thing or that, and never satisfied" (A1, 6, 6).

On a larger scale, the morning paper and the nightly news describe the damage done every day to persons, families, nations, and the international community by disordered desires for power, wealth, security, fame, and pleasure. The more we follow disordered desires, the more seriously we damage our personalities, ending in disruption of our fundamental relationships. "It is sad to consider," John observes, "the condition of the poor soul in whom [disordered appetites] dwell. How unhappy it is with itself, how cold toward its neighbors, how sluggish and slothful in the things of God!" (A1, 10, 4).

Yet even slightly disordered appetites — "a small attachment one never really desires to conquer, for example, to a person, to clothing, to a book or a cell, or to the way food is prepared, and to other trifling conversations and little satisfactions in tasting, knowing, and hearing things, and so on" (A1, 11, 4) — can seriously damage our soul by being an obstacle to spiritual progress and transformation in God.

John illustrates this by a bird tied to the ground with a thin thread. The thread may be easier to break than a heavy rope, but until it is finally broken, the bird cannot fly free. Neither are we free for perfect union with God in love as long as we are bound by disordered desires.

Thus, every disordered desire, however small, has the potential power to remove God's grace from our soul and to destroy our personality. For this reason, all who seek union with God must make purification of these appetites a priority. We must mortify — literally, put to death — our disordered desire for sensory pleasure produced by created objects. John reminds spiritual masters that their chief concern with their disciples is the "immediate mortification of every [disordered] appetite. These guides should make them remain empty of what they desire so as to liberate them from so much misery" (A1, 12, 6).

Counsels

John tells us how to do this. He gives specific counsels for centering our appetite, affection, and desire primarily in God. His advice is essential for beginners in the spiritual life, but remains valid for the entire journey.

The first counsel is to "have a habitual desire to imitate Christ in all your deeds by bringing your life into conformity with his. You must then study his life in order to know how to imitate him and behave in all events as He would" (A1, 13, 3).

Jesus is God's perfect self-communication to us. To act in all things as Jesus would is to act in union with God's will. This is especially true in mortifying our disordered appetite for sensory pleasure. Jesus' "meat and food" (Jn 4:34) was to do his Father's will. When our love of Jesus inspires us to seek God's will in everything, especially in things that provide pleasure to our senses, we bring order to our sensory desires.

John gives an example: "If you are offered the satisfaction of hearing things that have no relation to the service and glory of God, do not desire this pleasure or the hearing of these things.... And so on with all the other senses insofar as you can duly avoid such satisfaction." This practice purifies and empties the will of disordered desires for sensory pleasure and brings great spiritual progress in a short time (A1, 13, 4).

John's second counsel aims at establishing harmony and tranquility in our emotions. Like desire, emotions — joy, hope, fear, and sorrow — strongly affect our sensory life. He writes

Endeavor to be inclined always:

...not to the most delightful, but to the most distasteful;

...not to wanting something, but to wanting nothing.

Do not go about looking for the best of temporal things, but for the worst, and, for Christ, desire to enter into complete nakedness, emptiness, and poverty in everything in the world. (A1, 13, 6)

Practicing this counsel delivers us from our natural tendency to cling to pleasant experiences and to avoid unpleasant ones. Personally, it frees us to pursue truth and goodness, even when the price in self-denial is high. Socially and politically, it challenges power and progress as public priorities in favor of goals that benefit the real needs of people. Ultimately, this counsel centers our emotions in God. It helps us to rejoice "only in what is purely for God's honor and glory," hope for nothing else, feel sorrow only for what diminishes that glory, and fear only God (A3, 16, 2).

John's third counsel regards concupiscence — the desires of the flesh and eyes and the pride of life addressed in John the Evangelist's first epistle (1 Jn 2:16). "Try to act with contempt for yourself and desire that all others do likewise."[1]

This hard saying, like those of Jesus, strikes at the disordered relationship we establish with our own self. It seeks to establish an attitude of personal non-attachment that breaks overdependency on persons, places, and things to satisfy our emotional needs. The counsel attempts to free us from attachment to our own ego and self so that we may seek God's kingdom first (Mt 6:33).

John describes his final set of counsels for disciplining desire as instructions for journeying to union with God. These instructions are, in part, as follows:

> To reach satisfaction in all
> desire satisfaction in nothing.
> To come to possess all
> desire the possession of nothing....
>
> When you delay in something you cease to rush
> toward the all....
>
> And when you come to the possession of the all
> you must possess it without wanting anything.

Because if you desire to have something in all
your treasure in God is not purely your all.

(A1, 13, 11–12)

John's words here recall the Gospel paradox that is found
in nearly all mystical literature — to have all we must give
up all. God alone is the center of our lives, the sole purpose
for our existence. No thing can replace God in our lives. We
must not delay in anything, but seek God from the very first
movements of our hearts.

Therapy of Desire

John's counsels amount to a therapy of desire. They
all focus on desire: "desire to imitate Christ...," "endeavor to be inclined always: not to the easiest, but to
the most difficult...," "try to act with non-attachment to
yourself...," "to reach satisfaction in all desire satisfaction
in nothing."

The motive for working on our desires is love for Jesus
Christ, who exemplifies total fidelity to God's will, even
to dying naked on the cross, empty of all material possessions and deprived of every sensory pleasure. Imitating Jesus'
total self-emptying on the cross purifies our sensory life, inspires virtuous behavior, and leads us securely toward total
transformation in God. Overcoming our repugnance to these
counsels and practicing them faithfully with order and dis-
cretion eventually heals our soul, bestowing interior peace,
tranquility, delight, and consolation.

In this therapy, John intends, not the destruction of desire, but its transformation.[2] He attempts to help us become "recollected in one appetite alone, the desire for God"
(A1, 10, 1), which in practice means "the desire for the perfect fulfillment of [God's] law and the carrying of the cross of
Christ" (A1, 5, 8). Imitating Jesus in everything is to become
our one constant desire — *un ordinario apetito* (A1, 13, 3).

The mortification of disordered appetite thus means transforming our undisciplined desire for sensory pleasure into a focused desire for God alone, so that longing for God, rather than the pleasure provided by created things, motivates all our behavior. This single desire for God purifies our entire sensory life. It gradually transforms our disordered appetite for sensory pleasure into seeking "another, better love." Our pleasure now becomes following Jesus "with love's urgent longings" (A1, 14, 2). Our main concern is translating these longings into virtuous behavior that reflects the Gospel.

Purification of the senses means putting to death — mortifying — our desires for pleasures that arise from any other source than our longing for God. More purification still remains before one is fully transformed in God: faith must purify our spirit, contemplation our total being. But before describing these further purifications, let us see what parallels may be found in Buddhism to John's teaching on the mortification of appetites.

K.C.

Chapter 13

TEACHINGS OF THE BUDDHA

Purification of Conduct, the Gift of Morality

The Buddha said that to walk a spiritual path we must first consider conduct. Right speech, right actions, and right livelihood are the morality steps of the Buddha's noble eightfold path. Meditation practice greatly sharpens self-examination in these areas and can radically change how we look at what we do. When we harmonize conduct, we enjoy freedom from the suffering of harmful behavior.

Morality for Our Dark Side

The early Buddhist scriptures have a word for our dark side — *kilesa*. These problem-causing attitudes, feelings, and reactions make us unhappy when we experience them and can lead to inharmonious actions that harm others. *Kilesa* is commonly translated "defilement," referring to the impurity of such states. Scholars now say a truer translation is "torment of the mind."

The harm in cravings. One effect *kilesas* have on us is defilement, the common translation of *kilesa*. The *Dhammapada,* a collection of aphorisms attributed to the Buddha, says, "By oneself committing evil does one defile oneself; by oneself not committing evil does one become pure."[1]

The translation of *kilesa* as "torment of the mind" describes the Buddhist understanding that cravings torture us. They trap us in endless rounds of suffering, and the more intense they are, the greater the torment. "Beset by craving, the masses run about like an ensnared hare. Held fast by fetters, they come to suffering again and again for a long time."[2]

Cravings give us no rest; even if we satisfy them, desires again spring up and cause more thirst. This constant buffeting by desire is one special way in which earthly life is ultimately unsatisfactory.

Allowing desires to prevail increases delusion. "Fools... are enemies to themselves doing ill deeds that produce bitter fruit. ... So long as an evil deed has not yet born fruits, the fool thinks it as sweet as honey."[3] Craving blinds us. The more we allow it to reign, the more it co-opts our understanding into justifying and supporting it. We see things only as desire colors them, and can seriously deceive ourselves.

Finally, cravings make practicing virtue more difficult. The *Dhammapada* teaches, "Those who are corrupt do to themselves what only an enemy might wish for them. Easy to do are things that are bad and harmful to oneself. But exceedingly difficult it is to do that which is good and beneficial."[4]

The importance of *sila*.   When a monk asked the Buddha for spiritual guidance, the Buddha replied: "First establish yourself in the starting point of wholesome states, that is, in purified moral discipline and in right view." The morality path steps, called *sila,* are the necessary basis for the other parts of the path. *Sila* is our starting place in the work to overcome *kilesas,* to free ourselves from the grip of desires. *Nibbana* — the home toward which Buddhist practice aims — is sometimes even defined as putting out the fires of desire.

The behaviors we choose all bend our character ever so slightly in one direction or another. There is no such thing as "just this once won't count." So the training in *sila* involves self-restraint. We abstain from unskillful acts that cause suffering, and cultivate skillful action. Moral conduct brings peace and harmony to the mind, relationships, and society. It protects our dealings with others, prepares the mind for meditation practice, and frees us from guilt, shame, blame, and remorse.

Right Livelihood

Traditionally, right livelihood deals with how people earn a living. In the Buddha's time, how you earned a living determined almost all the rest of your lifestyle. Today, people engaged in the same livelihood choose many different lifestyles. Since lifestyle sets the framework in which our entire life unfolds, we must understand right livelihood more broadly.

Work. The work we do *is* a very important part of total lifestyle. Buddhist teachings prohibit work that makes suffering or harms others. Dealing in five objects is considered unskillful: weapons, living beings, meat, intoxicants, and poisons. So also is any wrong conduct in earning a living; this includes acts like cheating, usury, deception, flattery, harassment, and bribes. We are not to use "low worldly knowledges"; we do not offer people what is useless, induce desires in them for our own gain, or use coercive advertising. Finally, we are to respect all persons and objects involved in our work.

We ought choose work that we see as good or necessary to do. Work chosen only for extrinsic reasons — such as ease, money, convenience, privileges — will not provide a satisfying basis for life. Vietnamese Buddhist monk Thich Nhat Hanh, whom Martin Luther King nominated for the Nobel Peace Prize, developed conduct guidelines for contemporary people. He said: "Do not live with a vocation that is harmful to humans and nature. Do not invest in companies that deprive others of their chance to live. Select a vocation which helps realize your ideal of compassion."[5]

Lifestyle. Besides work, many other activities determine lifestyle. Avoiding actions with destructive potential is most important. Intoxicants, luxury, ambition, stinginess, and overindulgence in pleasures lead to trouble. These things can cause illness, and predispose the mind to heedlessness, restlessness, dullness, and unkindness.

Nhat Hanh also speaks to this. "Do not accumulate wealth while millions are hungry. Do not take as the aim of your life fame, profit, wealth or sensual pleasure. Live simply and share time, energy and material resources with those who are in need."[6] Nhat Hanh's precepts clearly touch issues that we could avoid by narrowly focusing on morality as defined in simpler times. He forces us to be accountable in often uncomfortable, but clearly necessary, ways if we honestly try to live appropriately in today's world.

We ought test our lifestyle's rightness for one committed to spiritual living. Ask where it falls on such dimensions as luxury versus temperance, stinginess versus generosity, ambition and competition versus cooperation, and moderation versus indulgence. When we bring a bare simplicity to how we live, we establish ourselves in right livelihood. We develop living patterns that dispose us to virtue rather than problem-causing speech and behavior.

Right Speech

We often overlook how very important speech is. Outer speech can cause considerable harm and suffering, but inner speech precedes all outward behavior. Intentions form in the mind before any action takes place. Habits of right speech with others help the mind develop right inner speech. The Buddha named four important considerations in speech.

Lying. Truthfulness is the first right speech. Something that is not true simply should not be said. Lying brings suffering to both liar and person lied to. It destroys trust, creates a tangled web to defend, and finally causes delusion when we believe our own lies. Non-lying is commitment to what is real, is choosing fact over desire-fueled fantasy. To truly follow the Buddha's path to satisfaction, we must always monitor speech for truthfulness.

When we avoid *deliberate* lies, we start seeing many ways we shade the truth without realizing it until afterward. Then we begin catching ourselves in the act of these small exaggerations, self-justifications, and self-glamorizings. I have not yet sat a long *vipassana* retreat in which I did not tell the teacher such an inadvertent lie. A helpful practice for this, when I catch myself doing it, is to confess the lie and tell the truth.

We also start seeing how we lie to ourselves to avoid the discomfort of recognizing our true motives, attitudes, and expectations. Because we think we are really truthful, seeing all these tendencies in ourselves can be very painful. However, it would be a rare person in whom they are not present.

Slander or tale-bearing.   The second wrong speech is causing dissension or separation among people. Slander or tale-bearing is often fueled by envy, resentment, or self-seeking. It disrupts relatedness and destroys unity. Creating a rift in the spiritual community is one of the more serious moral failures in Buddhist thought. Nhat Hanh singled this issue out: "Do not utter words that can create discord and cause the community to break. Make every effort to reconcile and resolve all conflict, however small."[7] Opposed to slander is speech that promotes good feeling, friendship, and harmony among people.

Harsh speech.   The third wrong speech is unnecessarily harsh speech. This usually occurs in intense emotion and is less serious than premeditated slander. However, it springs from anger and aversion, and creates unhappiness. Its antidote is patience, tolerating unpleasant situations without lashing out.

Idle speech.   The fourth wrong speech is idle speech, speech that is untimely or not useful. This guideline does not rule out affectionate talk between intimates, polite conversation with acquaintances, or speech needed to get work done. Much talk at offices, parties, and night spots, however, is idle speech. One Buddhist teacher said that quitting talking about other people eliminated over 90 percent of his speech.

The teachings list thirty-two categories of unprofitable speech. These give us an almost humorous way to examine how much we speak idly. They are speech about: rulers, criminals, government employees, armies, dangers, battles, food, drink, clothing, dwellings, adornments, perfumes, relatives, vehicles, villages, towns, cities (talk about sports teams, maybe?), provinces, the opposite sex, heroes, streets, baths, relations who have died, this and that, the origin of the world, the origin of the ocean, views about eternity, views about annihilation, worldly loss, worldly gain, self-indulgence, and self-mortification. Is there much left to talk about?

Other considerations.   In thinking about right speech, we should also think about listening. Do we listen to slander or idly spend hours with television or read junk fiction? Do we turn to a Walkman, boom-box, or radio to fill the environment with distracting and useless noise? Spending an evening alone without any speech, music, or reading is an interesting experiment.

Nhat Hanh also emphasized the importance of speaking when speech is needed. His speech precept reads: "Do not say untruthful things for the sake of personal interest or to impress people. Do not utter words that cause division and hatred. Do not spread news that you do not know to be certain. Do not criticize or condemn things that you are not sure of. Always speak truthfully and constructively. Have the courage to speak out about situations of injustice, even when doing so may threaten your own safety."[8]

Right Action

Right action means to avoid three types of behavior: killing, stealing, and sexual misconduct. Such actions create an enormous amount of suffering.

Killing. Killing any sensate being is prohibited; this includes even insects, those beings that crunch if we step on them or that whir around our heads. Deliberate harming, like assault, torture, or maiming, is also prohibited. Thich Nhat Hanh's rendering reads: "Do not kill. Do not let others kill. Find whatever means possible to protect life and to prevent war."[9]

Working with this path step requires carefully assessing our attitudes on many life issues. In the controversies that rage over some, such as abortion, suicide, and euthanasia, others often seem forgotten. These include war, civil rights, health care, and basic life necessities like food and shelter for the needy. We cannot forget these in developing reverence for life.

Stealing.   The second wrong action is taking what is not given — interesting wording that says more than merely not stealing. It suggests that we should not borrow anything without permission, nor assume the right to use anything unless clearly meant for us. What havoc following this simple practice would eliminate from family life in many homes! No one would ever have to wonder who borrowed their missing scissors or what happened to the tape that disappeared from their desk.

This guideline also prompts us to consider *failing* to give to others what *should* be given to them. Nhat Hanh's advice reads: "Possess nothing that should belong to others. Respect the property of others, but prevent others from enriching themselves from human suffering or the suffering of other beings."[10] If other people need things we own, how much of what we are not actively using is it right for us to possess? Do not material goods properly belong to those who need them, rather than those able to accumulate more than they can use? If a year goes by without her wearing an article of clothing, one woman says it no longer belongs to her. She gives it away to someone who will use it.

Sexual misconduct.   Buddhist texts list two main sexual misconducts. One is breaking a sexual commitment — in other words, adultery. The second is sexual activity with inappropriate other persons. This includes close family members, people vowed to celibacy, and vulnerable people unable to give free consent, like children or prisoners. We should add to these people mentally or emotionally impaired people and those over whom we exercise power, such as employees, students, or clients.

Sexual misconduct is broadly defined as using sexuality in a way that harms oneself or any other being. Much is implied in this; it certainly rules out all manipulation, force, deceit, trickery, or irresponsibility in sexual behavior. It should rule out the terrible problems of unwanted pregnancies and sexually transmitted disease.

Nhat Hanh looks at sexual conduct very broadly. "Do not mistreat your body. Learn to handle it with respect. Do not look on your body as only an instrument. Preserve vital energies (sexual, breath, spirit) for the realization of the Way. Sexual expression should not happen without love and commitment. In sexual relationships, be aware of future suffering that may be caused. To preserve the happiness of others, respect the rights and commitments of others. Be fully aware of the responsibility of bringing new lives into the world. Meditate on the world into which you are bringing new beings."[11]

Precepts

These path steps of right speech, right action, and right livelihood are the training in morality. These are not commandments, but guidelines saying what actions create suffering.

We freely train ourselves to avoid them. We recognize that our choices affect not only ourselves, but all beings and all things. The ripples created by dropping a small pebble into a large pond may be subtle, but they become increasingly wider until the entire pond is affected by them.

These training guidelines of *sila* are formalized in five precepts that all Buddhists are to observe. Others typically undertake the precepts while doing intensive meditation practice. They are helpful to anyone wanting to purify the heart. Perhaps you will be moved to live by them.

The first precept is not to kill — so it can become a "befriend a bug" exercise. You can remove it from your territory if you don't want to live with it, but you do not kill it. The second precept is not to take what is not given to you.

The third precept of avoiding sexual misconduct has a special meaning for intensive spiritual practice; retreatants are fully celibate, even regarding solitary sexual acts. The fourth precept against wrong speech also has a special retreat meaning — observing the "noble silence." Meditators speak only at designated times, such as with the teacher or when a real need must be tended.

The fifth precept is to refrain from intoxicants or mind-altering substances. This precept keeps the mind clear enough to be conscientious about the other precepts. Prescription medicines needed for health may be taken. I gave up my occasional glass of wine after my teacher told me it makes a difference in meditation practice; he was right.

We undertake these trainings as a gift to both ourselves and others. If you have ever been with someone whose integrity seems absolutely unshakeable, you know the comfort and security you felt. We seek to become that kind of being. The happiness we find is more deeply satisfying than what any unskillful behavior we have renounced could give us. May we all benefit from the commitment we make to observing basic morality.

M.J.M.

Chapter 14

ST. JOHN
AND THE BUDDHA
ON PURIFICATION
OF CONDUCT
Integrative Summary

The teaching of St. John of the Cross on the purification of disordered appetites and the Buddhist doctrine of the purification of moral conduct reveal some striking similarities that have important implications for spiritual practice.

Human Darkness

First of all, both John of the Cross and the Buddha share a common understanding and experience of the dark side of human nature. John writes of disordered appetites that torment, weaken, blind, and defile us. The Buddha speaks of cravings that torment the mind. Both agree that our inordinate cravings for sensual pleasure create suffering and disharmony in our relationships on all levels: personal, societal, universal, and cosmic. A quick perusal of the daily newspaper or a few minutes listening to the evening news on the television verifies the havoc and pain born in our personal and collective lives from our attachments to such things as alcohol, material possessions, codependent relationships, power, and prestige. According to the Buddha and John of the Cross, we need liberation from the disordered desires that prevent us from experiencing the fullness of life for which we were created.

Meditation and Life: A Unity

Their teaching on the need for purification of conduct and disordered appetites points to a second but related similarity. As all mystics of the major world religions, John and the Buddha emphasize that meditation and life go hand in hand; they form a unity. We cannot pray seriously and at the same time malign our sisters and brothers or engage in self-destructive behavior. The meditative life calls for total dedication to God and service to our neighbor expressed in concrete behavior. Therefore, spiritual practice demands a conscious ordering of our moral conduct, which requires on our part a serious discipline in the way we relate to God, others, and the world around us. John refers to this discipline as "mortification" of the appetites. Buddhism speaks of it as *sila*.

Spiritual Discipline

Herein lies another similarity between John of the Cross and the Buddha. Both offer counsels and guidelines that serve as a concrete, spiritual discipline to uproot selfishness and to bring about peace and harmony within ourselves and our relationships.

John places at the center of his counsels the person and life of Jesus Christ. "Have a habitual desire to imitate Jesus Christ in all your deeds by bringing your life into conformity with his" (A1, 12, 3). Any reformation of behavior or discipline we take on to purify ourselves is born from a personal relationship of love with Jesus Christ and rooted in imitation of his life.

Furthermore, John offers some maxims that contain a method for mortifying disordered desires and establishing tranquility and harmony in our emotional life. "Endeavor to be inclined always: not to the easiest, but to the most diffi-

cult; not to the most delightful, but to the most distasteful"
(A1, 13, 6). Although John's advice may seem a bit abstract
at a first reading, deeper reflection on his life and a broader
understanding of his doctrine reveal that he challenges us to
actively work toward uprooting selfish attitudes and behavior patterns that go contrary to Gospel values. The way we
live out these counsels depends upon the uniqueness of our
personality and our life situation.

Buddhism also offers a well-tried morality path. The path
of *sila* presents concrete precepts that, if taken seriously
and integrated in daily life, provide a tangible discipline for
interior transformation and peaceful and harmonious relationships. Right livelihood, right speech, and right action
produce concrete guidelines to cultivate simplicity of life and
selfless, loving relationships. For a Christian who may feel
puzzled by some of John's abstract maxims and wonder how
to apply them in daily life, the five precepts of *sila* have
ramifications that contain a sound and practical method of
entering into the self-emptying process about which John
writes in his counsels.

God's Healing Light

Finally, through insight meditation we become aware of the
inordinate desires and attachments that create so much suffering in our personal and collective lives. We see clearly the
torments of our minds and hearts. In the depths of silent
meditation, God's healing light shines in the darkest cor-
ners of our hearts and exposes and heals our addictions
and disordered relationships. In clear and simple awareness,
the possibility exists for God's love to heal and purify our
conduct.

D.C.

Section Two

The Second Level of Purification

MENTAL CONTENTS

Chapter 15

ST. JOHN OF THE CROSS
Purification of the Intellect, Memory, and Will

"To undertake the journey to God," writes John of the Cross in an early chapter of *The Ascent of Mount Carmel*, "the heart must be burned with the fire of divine love and purified of all creatures" (A1, 2, 2). We explained in chapter 12 how mortifying our disordered desires for created things purifies us at the level of sense. This chapter describes how faith purifies us at the level of spirit. In chapter 18, we will show how contemplation, the fire of divine love, burns, illumines, purifies, heals, and transforms the heart, uniting us with God in the Trinitarian life of love.

The Journey to Who We Are

In seeking union with God we seek to become fully who we already are. John of the Cross maintains that all human beings, even the world's greatest sinners, are united with God. Without God's creative power sustaining us from moment to moment, we would cease to exist. In this "substantial union," God is fully present in the very substance of our being sustaining us in existence.

Our purpose in life is to journey from this unconscious substantial union, which always exists even though we are unaware of it, to a fully conscious "union of likeness." This union comes about only through love, a conformity of the human and divine wills "so that nothing in the one is repugnant to the other." When we rid ourselves of what is repugnant and unconformed to God's will, we are "transformed in God through love" (A2, 5, 3). We become God through participation in God. Like Balaam, the Old Testament soothsayer, we "hear what God says, know what the Most High knows, and see what the Almighty sees" (Nm 24:2–17).

To arrive at this conscious union of likeness with God, we must do more than purify our sensory life through mortification of disordered desire; we must also purify our spirit through faith. John calls faith a "certain and obscure habit of soul" that enables us to believe divinely revealed truths that exceed natural human understanding (A2, 3, 1). Accepting God's self-revelation on divine authority rather than on the natural light of reason purifies our spirit and prepares us to eventually see God who alone "is the substance and concept of faith" (C1, 10). Faith leads us to God. In this life, we know God obscurely, through limited concepts, images, and human experiences; but, in the next life, we see God clearly, directly, and face-to-face.

Faith, Hope, and Love

Our "spirit" permits us to know and love others and to be in personal communion with God. This communion is possible because our spirit possesses intellect, memory, and will, powers that enable us to know and love and to receive God's self-revelation to us. Faith, together with hope and love, purifies these spiritual powers for union with God. Faith purifies intellect, hope purifies memory, and love purifies will.

This spiritual purification is not an arbitrary exercise; God's very being demands it. Ultimately, God is transcendent, totally inconceivable and unimaginable, completely beyond human experience. No human thought, understanding, image, feeling, or emotion is able to "apprehend" or capture God. Faith, hope, and love purify our attachment to inadequate concepts, images, and emotional experiences of God so that our spirit is free to be united with Incomprehensible Goodness and to receive all of God's self-communication to us. Until this purification is complete, we are not fully transformed in God, no matter how humanly profound our thoughts of God, compelling our images, or emotionally intense our religious experiences.

Besides preparing us for transformation in God, purifying our spirit in faith, hope, and love also heals our personality when it has been damaged by the effects of sin present in our relationships with others. Faith, for example, can free us from a distorted image of God as a punitive parent that keeps us imprisoned in neurotic fear and guilt. Hope can release us from painful memories that bind us emotionally to negative experiences of the past and lead us to childish reactions to present problems. By choosing to love God first in everything, love can heal dysfunctional human relationships. "I never got it right with my wife and kids," reported one recovering alcoholic, "until I started getting it right with God."

Counsels

To help us purify our spirit, John offers detailed advice for working with thoughts, memories, images, and emotions so that they do not become obstacles on the journey toward union with God. We might call his advice "active faith" because it stresses what *we* do to prepare our spirit for God; in the next section on contemplation, we speak of "passive faith," or accepting what *God* does in us to prepare us for divine union.

John teaches that, because God transcends human knowledge, we must never rest completely in our present understanding of God as though we have intellectually "captured" or comprehended God. God is always more than our present concept of God. We must always remain open to receive God's further self-revelation until we see God face-to-face in eternity.

"Souls must go to God," John writes, "by not comprehending rather than by comprehending, and they must exchange the mutable and comprehensible for the Immutable
and Incomprehensible" (A3, 5, 3). Our present knowledge
of God that comes through nature, revelation, and contemplation may be perfectly true, but is always incomplete.
Attachment to this incomplete knowledge can become an
obstacle to receiving what God wants further to reveal to us.

"I just don't know any more," a contemplative nun of
many years once told me. "I always thought I knew who God
was, but the longer I live and the more I pray, the more I
realize God is completely different than anything I ever imagined." She was discovering the truth of John's words that we
"must journey by knowing God through what God is not
rather than through what God is" (A3, 2, 3). She was experiencing the "exchange" of the "comprehensible" for the
"Incomprehensible." Clinging to her earlier understanding of
God would only slow her spiritual progress.

Surprisingly, the counsel of non-attachment holds even for
special hidden knowledge which we receive passively from
God. Attachment to these special communications delays
our journey to God and can create harmful attitudes like
pride and self-satisfaction. "People should be extremely careful always to reject this knowledge," John writes, "and they
should desire to journey to God by unknowing.... The effect
God desires to produce through these passive communications will be fixed in the soul without need for efforts of
its own... [I] insist on rejection of all this knowledge as a
control against any error" (A2, 26, 18).

Similarly, John gives a "general rule of conduct" (A3, 15,
chapter title) for purifying the memory. Because intellect
and memory are closely associated in human knowing, the
method is nearly identical to that for purifying the intellect.
He writes:

As often as distinct ideas, forms, and images occur to
[persons], they should immediately, without resting in

them, turn to God with loving affection, in emptiness of everything rememberable. They should not think or look on these things for longer than is sufficient for the understanding and fulfillment of their obligations, if these refer to this. And then they should consider these ideas without becoming attached or seeking gratification in them, lest the effects of them be left in the soul. Thus people are not required to stop recalling and thinking what they must do and know, for, if they are not attached to the possession of these thoughts, they will not be harmed. (A3, 15, 1)

Aware that this counsel may strike some as iconoclastic, John insists that he is not minimizing holy images, whether exterior ones like sacred icons or interior ones held in our memory; rather, he is "explaining the difference between these images and God." He continues his defense: "Images will always help individuals toward union with God, provided that no more attention is paid to them than necessary for this love, and that souls allow themselves to soar — when God bestows the favor — from the painted image to the living God, in forgetfulness of all creatures and things pertaining to creatures" (A3, 15, 2).

Finally, John teaches us how to purify the will, the spiritual faculty that enables us to love. The will invests all the strength of the soul — intelligence, memory, desires, feelings, emotions — in what we love. We purify the will when, in response to God's unconditional love for us, we continually choose to center our lives in God rather than in other persons, wealth, status, individual talents, charismatic gifts, religious experiences, or whatever else may attract us.

John states his guiding principle for purifying the will when discussing the emotion of joy: "The will should rejoice only in what is for the honor and glory of God" (A3, 17, 2). He then applies this principle to purifying the will of its attachment to temporal goods such as money, position, power, influence, and family. "At the first movement of joy toward things, the spiritual person ought to curb it, remembering the principle we are here following: There is nothing worthy of a person's joy save the service of God and the procurement of God's honor and glory in all things. One should seek this alone in the use of things, turning away from vanity and concern for one's own delight and consolation" (A3, 20, 3).

Paradoxically, this non-attachment heightens rather than destroys appreciation for and sensitivity to creation. We experience a "spiritual joy, a hundred times greater," from continually lifting our minds and hearts to God in the presence of breathtaking beauty, stirring music, delightful fragrances, delicious food, delicate touches and whatever else delights our senses. "Anyone who fails to conquer the joy of appetite will fail to experience the serenity of habitual joy in God by means of God's creatures and works.... [Only the person]... of pure heart finds in all things a joyful, pleasant, chaste, pure, spiritual, glad, and loving knowledge of God" (A3, 26, 5–6).

Such acts of faith, hope, and love purify our spirit for union with God. They create within us an attitude of non-attachment to our concepts, memories, images, feelings, and emotions, especially those that pertain to God. This attitude of non-attachment frees our spirit to respond to God's movement in our lives leading us to divine union. We train ourselves to be continually mindful of the first movements of our intellect, memory, and will. We learn to quietly center these movements in God while interacting with the persons and events of our lives. We open our lives completely to God.

Jesus Christ:
Faith's Object, Model, and Reward

Christian faith is, above all, an interpersonal relationship with God. We understand faith's purification of our spirit better when we see Jesus Christ as faith's object, model, and reward. John of the Cross imagines that were we to ask God for personal favors like private visions or revelations to help us on our way to divine union, God could respond in these words. "If I have already told you all things in my Word, my Son, and if I have no other word, what answer or revelation can I now make that would surpass this? Fasten your eyes on him alone because in him I have spoken and revealed all and in him you will discover more than you ever ask for and desire.... Hear him because I have no more faith to reveal or truths to manifest" (A2, 22, 5).

We discover more than we ask for or desire in Jesus because he is incomprehensible mystery, always more than our deepest understanding of him. Yet he is also our way to union with God through love. His example teaches us how to purify sense and spirit. He models the death to self that is necessary for our lives to be transformed in God.

"A person makes progress," John insists, "only by imitating Christ, who is the Way, the Truth, and the Life [Jn 14:6].... Accordingly, I would not consider any spirituality worthwhile that wants to walk in sweetness and ease and run from the imitation of Christ... Christ is the way and... this way is a death to our natural selves in the sensory and spiritual parts of the soul" (A2, 7, 8–9).

From his own meditation on the Gospels, John pictures Jesus dead on the cross as totally naked, emotionally abandoned, completely empty in both sense and spirit. Yet, in that moment, Jesus wrought his greatest work, "the reconciliation and union of the human race with God through grace." In the cross, the "truly spiritual" come gradually to understand the "way (which is Christ) leading to union with God." They see that "their union with God and the greatness of the work they accomplish will be measured by their annihilation of themselves for God in the sensory and spiritual parts of their souls."

John concludes: "When they are reduced to nothing, the highest degree of humility, the spiritual union between their souls and God will be an accomplished fact.... The journey then does not consist in consolations, delights, and spiritual feelings, but in the living death of the cross, sensory and spiritual, exterior and interior" (A2, 7, 11).

Letting go of disordered attachments to objects of sense and spirit is our "living death of the cross." Yet, in this non-attachment, we discover a new presence of Christ within us. John illustrates this with an episode from Jesus' risen life (Jn 20:19–29). "He who entered the room of his disciples bodily while the doors were closed and gave them peace, without their knowing how this was possible, will enter the soul spiritually without its knowing how or using any effort of its own, once it has closed the doors of its intellect, memory, and will to all apprehensions" (A3, 3, 6).

We purify our spirit through non-attachment to concepts, memories, images, feelings, and emotions. Then Jesus Christ, faith's reward, awakens in the depth of our souls, removes our fears, fills us with peace, and draws us into deeper love. As our love for Jesus within us deepens, we feel more keenly the fire of his love purifying us and transforming us in wisdom and compassion.

Faith: A Dark Journey

The journey to union with God in love is thus a dark journey because we travel always in purifying faith. We know God, not solely by the light of natural reason or various religious experiences, but primarily by accepting God's self-revelation. The journey is dark also because we voluntarily undertake to purify and empty our sense and spirit of every disordered attachment that hinders God's purifying and transforming self-communication. This effort toward total self-emptying is our loving response to a God whose infinite love for us was expressed in Jesus' self-emptying death on the cross.

Yet, in dark faith and emptiness we also discover the Spirit of the Risen Lord present within us guiding our life, leading us to divine union. In this union, "God's spirit makes [persons] know what must be known and ignore what must be ignored, remember what ought to be remembered . . . and forget what ought to be forgotten, and makes them love what they ought to love, and keeps them from loving what is not in God." In this union, the first movements and operations of all our human faculties and operations become divine, "since they are transformed into divine being" (A3, 2, 9).

To be "transformed in divine being" is to become fully who we already are: persons united with God. The journey from our unconscious, "substantial union" to a conscious "union of likeness" based on love requires that we continually purify our spirit through active faith, hope, and love. It demands, further, a faith completely open to receive God's purifying and transforming love in contemplation. Before describing this contemplation, let us first see the Buddhist teaching on the purification of mental contents and the training of the mind.

                                                             K.C.

Chapter 16

TEACHINGS OF THE BUDDHA
Purification of Mental Contents, Training the Mind

The middle part of Buddhist spiritual practice is training the mind to be docile, purifying its contents. This brings a much more subtle happiness than sense delights or mental excitement; once it is deeply tasted, desire for grosser pleasures wanes. The steps on the noble eightfold path to this satisfaction are right effort, right mindfulness, and right concentration.

The meditation instructions tell us how to work with these steps in sitting and walking practice. To be in spiritual commitment, we must also live these disciplines daily. Life itself becomes a meditative work of training and purifying the mind.

Right Concentration

What we concentrate on, where we rest our attention, is food we give our minds. It "becomes" our minds, just as food we give the body becomes the body. One meditator said that her mind continually replayed scenes from soap operas for the first three weeks of a three-month retreat. She finally vowed never again to watch another soap opera and has kept this resolve.

Our culture considers it entertaining to watch stories full

of brutality, violence, lust, and greed. We cannot control what gets aired on the media, but we *can* choose what we invite into our own minds. Buddhists recommend three types of concentration objects: neutral ones, objects of suffering, and beautiful mind-states.

Neutral objects. Over our days, we often let our minds spin out, running wild through unimportant or even unwholesome ideas. Any time we start feeling scattered, we can check in with the breath for grounding. Before I started concentrating on sensations while walking to the office, that time was usually spent in idle thought.

We can use routine bodily movements for concentration practice — like brushing teeth, scrubbing in the shower, washing dishes, stirring a pan, or sweeping a floor. If this does not sound "spiritual" to you, reflect that it means open-handedly embracing life moment to moment, an attitude of spiritual surrender.

Unpleasantness and suffering. The second group of concentration objects — suffering ones — is not appealing to modern American mentality. Yet it helps to realize that life is not without limit, that someday we *will* die, and that passing pleasures do not give lasting satisfaction.

A psychotherapist friend keeps a small skull on his desk for perspective. People have very interesting reactions to it; some try hard not to see it, some shove it out of sight, and some ask him to remove it. Very few show fully appropriate reactions.

Daily life provides many objects of suffering upon which to concentrate. If we really pay attention to any newscast, tears of compassion can come. However, we usually block awareness of such suffering. How interesting that people become intensely engrossed in fictional suffering in TV dramas, and yet cannot attend to the very real suffering going on around them!

Thich Nhat Hanh considered being open to suffering very

important. He wrote: "Do not avoid contact with suffering or close your eyes before suffering. Do not lose awareness of the existence of suffering in the life of the world. Find ways to be with those who are suffering by all means, including personal contact and visits, images, sound. By such means, awaken yourself and others to the reality of suffering in the world."[1]

Beautiful states. The final concentration objects are inspiring and beautiful ones. These include virtues, devotional objects, and the "heavenly mind-states," which describe appropriate attitudes toward other people. Part of this is the *metta* practice explained in the last unit; you can also train yourself to wish others well throughout your day.[2]

The first heavenly mind-state is loving-kindness, universal friendliness, and good will toward all beings with no exception. This includes the underprivileged and powerless of any society, next-door neighbors, and also neighbors halfway around the world. It includes the elderly, the ill, pets, insects. It also includes those who wield power. The Buddha told his monks to extend loving-kindness to beings making trouble for them. It does not matter whether we find another being appealing or not; we are to treat all with the same loving-kindness.

The Buddha explained the wisdom of such good will: "Hatred is never overcome by hatred; hatred is overcome only by love."[3] A habit of loving-kindness can save us when we are pulled toward feeling ill will. The fruits of this practice will be seen in such caring actions as generosity and service.

The second heavenly mind-state is compassion, the right attitude toward beings who are suffering. Simply doing awareness practice, being with and exploring our own suffering, draws out compassion. As we realize the suffering in our own being and in all beings, we can be with the suffering of the whole. We feel with those who suffer and want to relieve the suffering we see.

Along with wisdom, compassion is one of the great wings

of the Buddha's teachings. Compassion is very different from pity or from anger over suffering. In pity we condescend, setting ourselves apart from the sufferer. Anger dulls ability to see clearly the sheer fact of suffering; it makes compassionately entering into it impossible.

Sympathetic joy is taking delight in the good that others enjoy. This hardest heavenly mind-state directly opposes envy and jealousy. Although human nature does not easily rejoice when someone else has advantages, even the smallest taste of sympathetic joy is an extremely beautiful feeling.

The fourth heavenly mind-state is equanimity. Although we wish others all the loving-kindness, compassion, and sympathetic joy in the world, our wishes alone will not bring them happiness. These wishes are effective only as others can receive such blessings, and that depends upon what they choose. With equanimity, we develop the peace of accepting this fact.

Right Mindfulness

Thich Nhat Hanh bridges the gap between concentration and mindfulness: "Do not lose yourself in dispersion and in your surroundings. Learn to practice breathing in order to regain composure of body and mind, to practice mindfulness and to develop concentration and understanding."[4] All the world's great spiritual traditions agree that seekers should always be mindful, should know what is going on. How can we *remember* to be mindful at all times? The Buddha helped us by naming four foundations of mindfulness. If we check these regularly, we become mindful.

Four foundations of mindfulness.   Mindfulness of the body means noticing *changes* that occur in the body. On entering a new situation, be aware of its odors, sounds, and sights — and of the body's reactions to these. Is there tightening or relaxing; is there a new sensation somewhere? Such awareness tells us how we are reacting to the situation and can prevent poor management. We ought also become aware of how the body feels during particular actions, such as eating and speaking. We can learn the effects on the body of particular entertainments.

The second foundation of mindfulness is feeling-tone. All experiences carry some feeling, ranging from very unpleasant through neutral to very pleasant. Our stronger pleasant or unpleasant experiences most often trigger our problem reactions — such as greed or anger or fear. Awareness of feeling-tone gives us an edge in self-management.

A third major area of mindfulness is mind itself and the "colorations" on it of our different moods, sets, emotions, and states of consciousness. The Buddha said to know when the mind is with or without greed, aversion, and delusion. Unwatched, these states get us into the most trouble. If we can see an emotion as it starts to develop, we can deal with it before it springs us into problem behavior.

The fourth area of mindfulness is the objects of experience: truths or realities. This includes all sense objects, the factors of mind that work for our benefit or loss, and the underlying truths about experiences, such as impermanence and unsatisfactoriness.

Insight practice requires that we focus attention on these basic realities. The mind, however, is very much in the habit of paying attention to its own creations. Buddhists call these mental creations conventional reality.

Conventional realities. Concepts and ideas, with which we form opinions and beliefs, are socially agreed upon conventions. These conventional realities are not "real" like the four foundations of mindfulness are. They are a potent problem in spiritual practice because we seldom realize that our thoughts about something are not the reality itself. My thought about a banana is not a banana, and if I spend all my time thinking about bananas, I will never directly encounter a banana. Truth can be fully grasped only in experience, not conceptually.

Buddhist practitioner Alan Watts explained our imprisonment in concepts. "If you try to capture running water in a bucket, it is clear that you do not understand it and that you will always be disappointed, for in the bucket the water does not run. To 'have' running water you must let go of it and let it run. The same is true of life and of God."[5]

Our persistent patterns of thoughts, the tapes we play and replay for ourselves, are our own creations, edited versions of experience. Thinking them when we are meditating closes down meditation. Living in conceptual understandings blocks out direct awareness of important truths.

We accept many notions without examining them. They can make it impossible for us to experience directly what is true. Truth cannot enter a full or closed mind. This understanding underlies the Buddha's teachings on faith.

The Buddha on faith.   The Buddha was very practical, and he realized that attachment to ideas is a serious problem in spiritual work. So, he said not to believe *anything* that *anyone* tells you, no matter on what authority, including what he himself said. If a spiritual teaching attracts you, try it out. See what you get from its practice, what fruits it bears in your life. As Jesus also said, we assess value by observing fruits. If they are good, then a teaching is worth following. If not, it should be discarded. We must verify in our own experience what we adopt. We should *never* affirm what we have not tested; suspending judgment is the appropriate response to all untried teachings.

Westerners often think faith a matter of conceptual beliefs and that strong faith means feeling very certain about these opinions. Alan Watts said that belief sucks the thumb that points to truth instead of following in the direction it indicates. Beliefs insist that reality is as we say it is, while faith is full openness to truth. "Belief clings, but faith lets go."[6] Faith must be open to truth, whatever it may be. The more beliefs or opinions we have, the more we insist that partic ular concepts are truth, the less we have the openness that faith demands.

Buddhists see faith as willingness to invest in spiritual practice, as confidence in value seen, not as opinions held. Jesus seems to have agreed with him, teaching that mere "lip service" is not enough. Faith increasingly develops by being confirmed over and again in the fruits of practice. Buddhist saints come to invincible faith that keeps them true to what they have realized.

Right Effort

Right effort has four parts. We *prevent* unwholesome mind-states from arising and get rid of unwholesomeness that *is* present. We encourage wholesome mind-states to arise and retain wholesomeness that *is* present.

Prevention. We want to prevent mind-states rooted in greed, aversion, or delusion. A major practice for this, sense restraint, does not mean withdrawal from experiences. If we are *mindful* of experiences and their feeling-tone, we are protected from being overcome by greed or aversion. If we are open to sensory events *without* mindfulness, they easily draw us into negativity. In the untrained mind, appealing objects draw out greed — the whole point of advertising. Unappealing objects elicit some form of aversion: anger, fear, or sadness.

When we can see sensory experiences as simple, passing phenomena, without getting caught up in such notions as *my* experience and *my* pleasure or pain, we have proper sense restraint. Lack of mindfulness is the problem, not experience itself. However, we should choose experiences wisely, for we all remain vulnerable until we reach a very high level of understanding.

Removing. To abandon a persistent unwholesome state, the Buddha said first to cultivate its opposite. When we obsess about feeling unjustly treated, anger arises. When we feel deprived, resentment or sadness follows. When we cultivate opposite attitudes, such as gratitude and surrender, unwholesome mind-states drop off. Thich Nhat Hanh recommends this method: "Do not maintain anger or hatred. As soon as anger and hatred arise, practice the meditation on compassion in order to deeply understand the persons who have caused anger and hatred. Learn to look at other beings with the eyes of compassion."[7]

Sometimes this proves too hard. Then we can develop inner revulsion to the negativity with two wholesome mind-states. Moral sensitivity shrinks from unwholesomeness as degrading and unworthy. Moral conscientiousness dreads doing anything that will cause harm, so pulls away from unwholesome attitudes. We must be careful in doing this not to fall into self-hatred. We develop revulsion to the unwholesome mind-state, not ourselves.

When I found myself frequently drawn into ugly gossip about a colleague, my teacher suggested a vow against such speech. I feared that I could not keep the vow, but he explained that it would make me more sensitive to "invitations" to backbiting before I was already into it. I would then more easily catch myself before the fact, rather than after. I broke the vow a few times, but promptly retook it. Eventually, seeing the ugliness of such speech released me from wanting to be part of the office group sharing it.

If cultivating revulsion fails, a third method is deliberately diverting attention to something else. We must carefully choose the object for this, so that we do not jump from the frying pan into the fire. One meditator bothered with sleepiness in practice aroused feelings of lust to get rid of it. Of course, he wound up with more trouble than in the beginning.

A fourth way is to directly confront the unwholesome attitude. When carefully explored and examined, it loses its strength to move us and simply becomes an object of study. A friend who is prone to depressions once decided simply to stare depression in the face until it left. Although she is not a meditator, this solid method worked; the depression lifted in days rather than weeks.

The fifth method to get rid of unwholesome mind-states, deliberate and vigorous suppression of the unwholesome attitude, is drastic and should be used only if all else fails. Scriptural texts say that screwing up your face and biting your tongue can force the attitude away.

Many people feel they must openly express anger or depression to get rid of them, while the opposite is actually true. The more we act upon such states, the more we encourage them to stay around. It *is* important to recognize when they are present, not denying their existence, but absolutely *not* necessary to act upon them.

Developing. Two meditation methods develop wholesome mental states. Concentrative meditation focuses attention on the attitude we want to increase, such as loving-kindness. Awareness practice, which cultivates wisdom, brings with it beautiful and appropriate mind-states.

We can also develop wholesome states through daily choices. People tend to bring ideas and attitudes into line with behavior, so we can "prime the pump" by doing things that encourage wholesome states. For example, we can deliberately cultivate attitudes the Buddha called "great good fortune." These include reverence, a heart grateful for what it has received, and the humility of being "teachable" and learning from others. Simply doing actions that reflect such attitudes, "going through the motions," encourages the corresponding attitudes to arise.

We can also choose experiences that bring wholesome attitudes. Being willing to see suffering makes occasions for compassion. Seeing good in others arouses loving-kindness. We can change habits of focusing on what is "wrong" about others to noticing what is "right."

Maintaining.   Acting on wholesome mental states makes them habitual so that they will come more frequently and stay longer. One Buddhist teacher cultivated generosity by vowing to act on every serious thought of giving something. If we become aware when such wholesome states arise, and fully encourage them, we develop a mind more and more filled with them.

Summary

So, to purify mental contents, we have right effort, right mindfulness, and right concentration. In formal meditation practice, they train and purify the mind, making it receptive for wisdom. In everyday life, we can continue the effort. May we be moved to do so.

M.J.M.

Chapter 17

ST. JOHN AND THE BUDDHA ON PURIFICATION OF MENTAL CONTENTS
Integrative Summary

Throughout this book we discuss our need for purification and healing. As we work our way through the various levels of purification, we may lose sight of its purpose. Why undergo such self-knowledge and growth? Why expend so much energy on spiritual practice?

Both St. John and the Buddha would reply: because we were created for happiness and wholeness. The purification of mental contents explained in the previous two chapters has as its purpose our happiness and fulfillment.

Our Goal: Love, Wisdom, and Happiness

The writings of John of the Cross and the Buddha reveal a profound concern for us as beings created to love and be loved. According to John, our purpose in life is to journey from an unconscious "substantial union" with God to a conscious "union of likeness" whereby we love God, others, and creation with God's very own love. We were created to participate in God's life. Conscious, loving awareness of our union with God and sharing this love with others bring us abiding spiritual peace, joy, and health, even in the midst of suffering.

Buddhism's two great wings are wisdom and compassion. The Buddha said we are in an unconscious state of enslavement to cravings that create suffering and cloud clear seeing into the impermanent and unsatisfactory nature of life. He understood our vocation in life as a movement to a state of ever-deepening insight into the true nature of reality. Wisdom and compassion are born from this insight. They bestow upon us the blessings of interior freedom, happiness, serenity, and loving-kindness to ourselves and all beings.

Training for Wisdom and Love

Even though God created us for love and happiness, we find these difficult to attain. We carry a whole world inside us. Damaged images and inadequate concepts of God, painful memories of past hurts, powerful emotions such as anger, lust, jealousy, and fear lurk deep within our psyche and prevent us from enjoying the joy, peace, and love for which God created us and constantly offers us. John and the Buddha knew that so much unhappiness and suffering continue in our lives because we live unaware of this inner world and its influence in our personal and collective lives.

For this reason, they challenged us to train our minds and hearts for wisdom and love. They taught us the interior discipline of non-attachment to knowledge, memories, images, emotions, concepts, beliefs, ideas, and unwholesome mindstates that keep us from discovering truth. They offered us spiritual practices to help us empty ourselves of the mental contents that distort our vision of reality and prevent us from becoming who we are.

The Theological Virtues

For John of the Cross, the theological virtues of faith, hope, and love purify and heal our spirit. Through an active and living faith in God who transcends all concepts and images, we can surrender our inadequate and neurotic images of God. We can rest secure in the mystery of our incomprehensible God whom we trust loves us unconditionally and sustains us even in our brokenness and dark moments.

The virtue of hope empowers us to let go of painful, paralyzing memories. Past memories may imprison us emotionally and keep us from living whole, healthy, and mature lives. Hope helps us see God's hand in all life's circumstances, painful as well as joyful, and enables us to surrender our past to the merciful love of God.

John's doctrine on the purification of the will teaches us to become mindful of our deepest emotions and interior movements. Through conscious acts of loving, we mindfully choose to center our lives in God rather than to invest our emotions and energies in persons, wealth, status, and power in ways that fragment us.

To embrace the theological life of faith, hope, and love is to enter into the dying and rising of Jesus Christ. This path of discipleship requires an ever-deepening awareness of the interior movements of our minds and hearts so that we can let go of those concepts, images, emotions, and memories that prevent us from living in close communion with God, others, and the world around us.

Concentration, Mindfulness, and Effort

We find a similar path in Buddhism. Right concentration, right mindfulness, and right effort are spiritual disciplines that purify the mind and heart. Right concentration keeps us rooted in reality and helps us to focus our minds on what is wholesome, truly compassionate, and loving. In holding the mind steadily on wholesome contents, right concentration purifies memory — a task John said is needed.

Right mindfulness trains us to become aware of what is going on around and within us. So many problems and sufferings arise because we live unaware of what we are feeling, thinking, and doing. Unmindful that we are angry, we may lash out at others before we can stop ourselves. A history of broken relationships may stem from deep unconscious feelings of insecurity that drive us to control others. Right mindfulness purifies the intellect by keeping us aware of our inner world and keeping us from investing energy needlessly in thoughts, concepts, and ideas.

Furthermore, the Buddha taught right effort as a means of determination and perseverance on the path. Becoming an enlightened person demands commitment and effort. Right effort demands cultivating wholesome thoughts and letting go of unwholesome ones such as anger, greed, and jealousy. The Buddha's teaching on right effort resonates with Jesus' saying, "It is not those who say to me, 'Lord, Lord,' who will enter the kingdom of heaven, but the person who does the will of my Father in heaven" (Mt 7:21). Right effort also corresponds to John of the Cross's task of purifying the will of interior movements contrary to the honor and glory of God.

If practiced daily, the Buddhist discipline of right effort, right concentration, and right mindfulness plunges us into the process of dying to what brings suffering and unhappiness to our lives and rising to what bestows peace, love, and serenity. Like the theological virtues of faith, hope, and love they encompass a whole way of life and illustrate that meditation is more than an exercise we do once or twice daily. Rather, meditation is a way of being, a path of transformation.

The Value of Insight Meditation

Finally, the teachings of the Buddha and St. John of the Cross point to the value of insight meditation. This practice offers us a door to enter our interior world of images, concepts, emotions, and memories. It teaches us to be with these mind-states. Just as we see more clearly in a pool of water when it is calm and still, so in interior silence we begin to perceive the movements of our hearts and minds. As we grow in awareness of what fuels and motivates our lives, we journey steadily toward the happiness, peace, and love for which God created us.

D.C.

Section Three

The Third Level
of Purification

FRUITION

Chapter 18

ST. JOHN OF THE CROSS
Contemplative Purification

We have described the purification of sense and spirit through mortification and faith. However, a further purification is still necessary before we are united with and transformed in God through love. This is the purification of our entire being through contemplation. Why, if we have persevered in actively purifying sense and spirit, is more purification necessary? What obstacles to union with God still remain?

John of the Cross maintains that our desire for sensory pleasure is so strong and pervasive and our self-love so deep and subtle that we are incapable of purifying them by our own efforts alone. Only God can purify us of every obstacle to divine union. God does this through contemplation, God's intimate self-revelation and self-gift to us in love. Contemplation is divine loving knowledge that illumines and purifies our entire being. As fire transforms a log into itself, so God's self-communication purifies our hearts, heals all our wounds, and transforms us into the divine life of Trinitarian love.

The Pleasure Principle and Unconscious Motivation

Using the seven capital sins, John describes how the pleasure principle motivates beginners on the spiritual journey. Even though their conversion to the spiritual path is real and their desire to love and serve God is genuine, subtle forms of spiritual pride, avarice, lust, gluttony, envy, anger, and sloth continue to inspire their behavior, especially their religious exercises.

Some undertake meditation and other spiritual exercises primarily because of the feeling of well-being they receive from these practices; others involve themselves in social causes to express their unrecognized anger with authority. Even those who have progressed into higher stages of prayer continually discover that their conscious self-sacrifice for others is often motivated by a previously unnoticed need for acceptance and approval. They eventually recognize how their unconscious needs move them, but feel helpless, despite continual prayer and mortification, to discover and purify their real motives and change their behavior. The deep roots of their disorder are hidden from their eyes.

Through contemplation, God purifies our persistent desire for sensory pleasure and the barriers to divine union alive in our unconscious. John describes contemplation as "an inflow of God into the soul, which purges it of its habitual ignorances and imperfections, natural and spiritual." This infused contemplation, which is God's own "loving wisdom," secretly and painfully teaches us "the perfection of love." By illuminating and purifying all our motives, contemplation prepares us "for union with God through love" (N2, 5, 1).

Contemplation is God's most intimate self-revelation to us. Nature reveals God's beauty, majesty, and power. Scripture and tradition reveal God as Trinity of Persons, as Incarnate in Jesus Christ. In contemplation, God communicates with us as a personal friend. For John of the Cross, Jesus, the total, complete, final self-revelation of God, was "a brother, companion, master, ransom, and reward" (A2, 22, 5). Jesus was the bridegroom of his soul for whom John felt "love's urgent longings." John imagined Jesus as sleeping "upon my flowering breast which I kept wholly for him alone" (A, poem, stanzas 1, 6).

John believed that he was able to reach "the sweet and delightful life of love with God" because of "the strength and warmth [his soul] gained from loving its Bridegroom in this obscure contemplation" (N1, explanation, 1–2). God's self-communication in contemplation is like the mutual self-revelation of human lovers in the growth and expressions of their love.

Prayer

We open ourselves to receive God's self-communication through prayer, which is a conscious centering of our minds and hearts in God, concerned to please God alone.[1] Prayer ordinarily develops through two stages. It begins with discursive meditation and, usually after a relatively short time, passes on to contemplation. Prayerful reflection or discursive meditation is our work for God; contemplation is God's work in us.

Discursive meditation is a prayer for beginners on the spiritual journey. It relies heavily on our senses and imagination to bring sensory delight and emotional involvement in the object of meditation. From this sensory and emotional experience comes pleasure in the idea of God and courage for serving God. By contrast, contemplation, the prayer of those more advanced along the spiritual journey, is centered in the spirit, a quiet receiving of God's loving knowledge in our intellect, memory, and will.

Discursive meditation prepares us for contemplation; contemplation brings us to union with God in love, a state of being in which prayer becomes a continuous act of love. However, before contemplation begins, we must first be purified of the subtle self-seeking that often motivates our discursive meditation and religious exercises.

Discursive Meditation

"The practice of beginners," John writes, "is to meditate and make acts and discursive reflection with the imagination" (F3, 32). Meditation for John is primarily a discursive practice. Using memory and imagination, we form mental images. With our reasoning, we reflect upon these images and other religious concepts and draw out implications for our daily lives. Examples of images John suggested for discursive meditation are "imagining Christ crucified or at the pillar or in some other scene; or God seated on a throne with resplendent majesty; or imagining and considering glory as a beautiful light, and so on..." (A2, 12, 3).

Involving our feelings and emotions in these images and concepts usually inspires fervent acts of love for God and resolutions to serve God faithfully. This discursive practice brings us "some knowledge and love of God" (A2, 14, 2). The delight and satisfaction arising from meditation enables us to disengage our desires from the attractions of the world and center them in God, preparing ourselves for God's self-communication in contemplation.

Dryness

Discursive meditation as a way of praying usually ends when we experience, sometimes suddenly after months of delightful communing with God, psychological and spiritual dryness. This dryness involves a loss of pleasure in the things of God and of the world, together with a sudden inability to meditate discursively, although the longing for union with God remains. The dryness occurs because God is beginning to communicate more directly to our spirit and less through our senses and imagination. Consequently, our sensory life begins to feel like a desert as God speaks more immediately to our spirit. "God...wishes to lead [spiritual persons] to more spiritual, interior, and invisible graces by removing the gratification derived from discursive meditation" (A2, 12, 6). If we choose to continue prayer in the midst of this emotional desert, the primary motive now becomes our faith and love for God rather than the pleasure prayer gives us. Dryness has purified our pleasure principle.

Transition to Contemplation

When these three phenomena — loss of pleasure, an increased longing for God, and an inability to meditate discursively — occur simultaneously, we know that God has
begun to "wean the soul... and place it in the state of contemplation" (F3, 32). At this point, John counsels a complete
change in the way we pray. We no longer need to reflect discursively on Gospel episodes or religious images; neither is it
important to derive emotional delight and satisfaction during
our periods of prayer. Such discursive activity now becomes
"an obstacle in the path of the principal agent who... is God,
who secretly and quietly inserts in the soul loving wisdom
and knowledge, without specified acts."

Instead, John advises that persons should now "proceed
only with a loving attention to God, without making specific
acts. They should conduct themselves passively... without
efforts on their own but with the simple loving awareness, as when opening one's eyes with loving attention"
(F3, 33).

In this quiet, passive, loving attention to God, we make
the transition from meditative or discursive prayer to contemplative prayer. Our challenge in prayer now is to be still
before God alive in the depth of our being with our minds
and hearts — our intellects, memory, and will — totally
open to receive God's self-communication in divine, loving
knowledge.

For years, our prayer may remain simple, quiet, peaceful,
and spiritually energizing, even in the midst of external activities and pressures. Nevertheless, despite this abiding peace,
our spirit is still not yet fully purified. In fact, the longer we
pray contemplatively, the more conscious we become of our
need for God to purify the deep roots of our self-love, roots
that we have become increasingly aware of, but feel helpless
to purify on our own.

Contemplative Purification

God eventually responds to our desire for purification with a more intense self-communication to us. We experience this communication interiorly as general, non-specific loving knowledge — light and heat together, like a fire. In the light of this knowledge, our awareness of God as Incomprehensible Goodness increases. Consciousness of the Risen Lord's loving presence within us grows steadily.

At the same time, we also see ourselves more clearly. In the light of God's love for us, we become vividly aware of the self-seeking in even our most altruistic activity. We wonder if we love God at all. Worse still, as we observe our incessant self-seeking, we wonder if even the all-good God can possibly love one so self-centered as ourselves. On the one hand, our longing for God deepens as we become more aware of the divine goodness; on the other, we fear never being worthy of God because of all the unhealed disorder we see in our own soul.

The growing awareness of God's love, the pain caused by our own self-knowledge, and the fear of God's loss now begin to cause us highs and lows psychologically. At times, we are deeply consoled and confident that God could never abandon us, only then, shortly afterward, to be cast down into helpless feelings of unworthiness and fear that God could never love us.

At other times, we feel lost at sea. We could never return to our former ways of living; yet, we wonder if God could possibly ever receive us. The thought of the future fills us with dread. In these emotional ups and downs, God finally purifies us of our deepest attachment to ourselves, heals our souls, and transforms us in the divine life of love.

We are purified, healed, and transformed in this emotional upheaval precisely because our "spiritual eye" gives us a "very clear picture" of ourselves. "A person's sufferings at this time cannot be exaggerated; they are but little less than the sufferings of purgatory." Through this interior suffering, however, God "heals the soul of its many infirmities, bringing it to health.... All the soul's infirmities are brought to light; they are set before its eyes to be felt and healed" (F1, 20–21).

Nothing remains hidden; the fears, delusions, compulsions, projections, and jealousies that subtly motivate our behavior are finally revealed to us. We recognize that for years we have been unconsciously working to establish our own illusory self rather than the kingdom of God. We are deeply embarrassed and ashamed to see all our inner workings; yet, we also trust that this painful awareness is healing us so that in everything we can live and act for God's honor and glory alone.

As this healing of our self-love nears completion, the emotional ups and downs lessen, a sign that the contemplative purification is nearly over. The "state of perfection," in which we are united with and transformed in God, is at hand. This state consists in the perfect love of God and complete non-attachment to self. Because this state demands both the knowledge of God and of self, we have necessarily been tried in both. Alternately we have been consoled in God's love and humbled by what we have discovered about ourselves. Finally, "the ascent and descent cease through the acquiring of perfect habits. For the soul will then have reached God and united itself with God" (N2, 18, 3–4).

Transformation in Divine Loving Wisdom

In his *Spiritual Canticle* and *The Living Flame of Love,* John describes the union of the human person with God in love with rich imagery and vivid detail. From the viewpoint of human purification, this union of love is primarily a union of the human and divine wills. For this reason, we experience transformation in God as a complete reformation of our motives. We are now moved to act, not by the satisfaction or dissatisfaction we find in persons, things, and events, but by the Holy Spirit.

Evoking Mary of Nazareth as the perfect exemplar of a

transformed human being because "she was always moved by the Holy Spirit" (A3, 2, 10), John writes: "The soul, like a true daughter of God, is moved in all by the Spirit of God, as St. Paul teaches in saying that those who are moved by the Spirit of God are children of God . . . [Rom 8:14]." Their intellect is God's intellect, their memory is God's memory, their will is God's will, their delight is God's delight. Although they always remain uniquely themselves without their substance ever becoming God's substance, they "become God through participation in God" (F2, 34).

Continually inspired by the Holy Spirit, the living flame of divine love, persons transformed in God are moved only by love. Everything they do is an "exercise of love." In loving God alone, they also love all beings unconditionally and unselfishly. They expend all their energies serving God and the Church.

They have lost interest in satisfying themselves or pleasing others out of mere human respect. The persistent demands of their ego to live an autonomous life apart from God's will have ceased. Their soul is in peace, like a "house at rest" (A, poem, stanzas 1, 2), no longer disturbed by conflicting desires and emotions.

They experience their breathing as one with the breath of God. John explains: "The Holy Spirit elevates the soul sublimely and informs her and makes her capable of breathing in God the same spiration of love that the Father breathes in the Son and the Son in the Father" (C39, 3).

In prayer, they have passed beyond all methods and simply enjoy communion with God in faith and love. They continually seek more solitude to deepen their "attentiveness to God and the continual exercise of love in God" (C29, 1). They are convinced that deepening this communion with God is their best way of serving God's people. They believe that "a little of this pure love is more precious to God and the soul and more beneficial to the Church, even though it seems one is doing nothing, than all . . . other works put together" (C29, 2).

John of the Cross: A Transformed Personality

When John exclaims poetically that the night of purgative contemplation "has united the Lover with his beloved, transforming the beloved in her Lover" (A, poem, stanza 5), it is hard to miss the autobiographical character of his words. Indeed, John exemplifies a human personality transformed in God's love.

People generally think of John as a man who removed himself from the stressful burdens of daily life to revel in extraordinary aesthetic and mystical experiences. While he always longed for deeper solitude, he in fact spent his adult years in nearly continuous administrative and educational service to his Carmelite brothers and sisters and in providing sacramental ministry and spiritual guidance to numerous people. He wrote his poetry and spiritual treaties only as he could find time in his busy schedule.

That such activity did not prevent his transformation in wisdom and compassion is perhaps best illustrated by an incident near the end of his young life. A Carmelite nun had written to him decrying the shameful plot of one of his Carmelite brothers to drive him from the order. In response, John wrote back: "Do not let what is happening to me, daughter, cause you any grief, for it does not cause me any.... Men do not do these things, but God, who knows what is suitable for us and arranges things for our good. Think nothing else but that God ordains all, and where there is no love, put love, and you will draw out love..." (L 26).

With divine wisdom, he interpreted events through the eyes of God; with divine compassion, he responded to people with the non-violent heart of Jesus Christ. The words John uses to describe a soul always moved by the Holy Spirit aptly apply to himself: "It seems to it that the entire universe is a sea of love in which it is engulfed, for conscious of the living point or center of love within itself, it is unable to catch sight of the boundaries of this love" (F2, 10).

Our purification ends in this state of union and transformation. It has come about, finally, because of God's self-communication to us and our own "passive" or receptive faith. In contrast to the "active" faith mentioned in chapter 15 on the purification of our spirit, passive faith is our openness to accept all that God desires to accomplish in us. Contemplation is thus not limited to times of formal prayer, but becomes the experience of life itself. We recognize God purifying, healing, and transforming us in every event of our lives.

Conclusion

John of the Cross taught that "here on earth, [persons] are cleansed and illumined only by love" (N2, 12, 1). God's total self-giving in Jesus Christ initiates this love; our total self-emptying of sense and spirit responds to this love. As we continually surrender ourselves to God through faith, mortification, and prayer, God's self-communication to us becomes more intense, transforming us gradually in divine being.

If we are faithful to God, God is faithful to us. John writes: "If individuals would eliminate these impediments [of sense and spirit] ... and live in pure nakedness and poverty of spirit, ... their soul in its simplicity and purity would then be immediately transformed into simple and pure Wisdom, the Son of God. As soon as natural things are driven out of the enamored soul, the divine are naturally and supernaturally infused since there can be no void in nature" (A2, 15, 4).

In the concluding Part IV of this book we shall discuss how insight meditation facilitates this transformation in Christ. Before that, however, let us look at the realization of wisdom and compassion in the Buddhist tradition.

K.C.

Chapter 19

TEACHINGS OF
THE BUDDHA

Purification of the Heart —
Wisdom, the Goal of Realization

Once the mind can remain still and contented, then the highest happiness can develop — the satisfaction of wisdom. Wisdom ripens fully only when behavior and mental contents have been purified. The path's wisdom steps are right understanding and right intention. Right understanding is the fruit of formal meditation practice and of earnest spiritual living in everyday life. From this realization comes right motivation, being a saintly presence in the world.

Barriers to Wisdom

Even when conduct and mental contents are relatively pure, subtle impurities remain. These are mostly not conscious, and rest on strongly conditioned tendencies of the heart.

Clinging to opinions. The Buddha said that clinging to opinions can keep us locked in the bondage of ignorance, making it difficult or impossible to see truth. Thich Nhat Hanh has a solidly Buddhist horror of dogmatism. His very first precept is: "Do not be idolatrous about or bound to any doctrine, theory, or ideology, even Buddhist ones. All systems of thought are guiding means; they are not absolute truth."[1]
We seldom realize when we are worshiping words because

we confuse concepts with that to which they point. We get very attached to comfortable understandings of ourselves, reality, others — even the Ultimate Reality. Holding onto favorite understandings often makes us feel very secure, but this "safety" rests on shifting sand, not firm reality.

Many consider clinging to opinions virtuous and fail to see the folly of this. We call it great strength when nothing can change our minds. From Thich Nhat Hanh: "Do not think the knowledge you presently possess is changeless, absolute truth. Avoid being narrow-minded and bound to present views. Learn and practice non-attachment from views in order to be open to receive others' viewpoints."[2]

Nhat Hanh pushes us even farther: "Do not force others, including children, by any means whatsoever, to adopt your views, whether by authority, threat, money, propaganda or even education. However, through compassionate dialogue, help others renounce fanaticism and narrowness."[3] I recall an old cartoon.[4] A Crusader sits high on a big white horse, holding his spear at the throat of an Arab spread-eagled on the ground. The caption reads: "Suddenly I'm very interested in this Christianity of yours. Tell me more."

Clinging to opinions blinds us into not seeing clearly and can lead people to do much evil in the guise of good. Opinions may make us feel secure, but can work against spiritual growth. We need to revise them as we understand more. As we willingly relinquish old opinions that have outlived their usefulness, we grow increasingly open to truth.

Underlying assumptions.   Assumptions are another problem. We often do not even know these, because they stay unconscious until we ferret them out. We unthinkingly accept much as true about the world, ourselves, and others. These presuppositions powerfully condition our behavior, so our choices reveal what we assume and expect. Since underlying assumptions often directly oppose what we know consciously, it requires some work to understand them.

For example, in spite of knowing that it leaves me feeling groggy, unmotivated, and out of sorts, sometimes I still reach for the second bowl of ice cream. We who use food unskillfully unconsciously accept overeating as a good choice; it must meet a deeply felt need. Perhaps we want to fill ourselves with something good to ward off guilt, or we might want more buffer between ourselves and the outside world. Understanding how we irrationally act against ourselves is part of being purified.

Similarly, how we react to changes in fortune tells us what is *binding* us, what we assume we absolutely need. Such attachments imprison us and keep us trying to hold on to what cannot be secured.

Because assumptions are deeply entrenched and unconscious, they are a harder task to address than conscious opinions. Meditation practice helps by baring much that we hide from ourselves. It can reveal an assumption's origin, most frequently in early life. Purification of these hidden, harmful tendencies of the heart breaks subtle chains that bind us.

Understanding the darker forces in our minds is a bridge to right motivation. Opinions and assumptions not only obscure our seeing of truth, but are also strong motivational forces.

Seeing motivations. Let us now do some diagnostic work on motives. Without such self-understanding, spiritual endeavor will not bear fruit. To what does the mind turn when not engaged in other activities? What does it spin out into?

Does the mind think of power, prestige, material gain, being loved, ambition, pleasures, or ease? Does it go to some specific "addiction," a particular substance or person or activity? Do we dwell in the past or future, or distance ourselves from the present by analysis, complaint, or spacing out? If we carefully watch in our sitting meditation and daily life, seeing where the mind goes will show us strong motivational forces in our lives.

Behind these conscious preoccupations are tendencies to

misuse experiences, relationships, and possessions. Any obsessive bent of mind almost always results in abuse. Not even spiritual aspirations are free of this. Do we sanctify as "spiritual yearnings" other motives like self-importance, control, or gain? Thich Nhat Hanh is sensitive to this: "Do not use the Buddhist community for personal gain, or transform your community into a political party. A religious community, however, should take a clear stand against oppression and injustice and should strive to change the situation without engaging in partisan conflicts."[5]

We are also motivated to protect ourselves from raw self-knowledge. Defense mechanisms are subtle, self-protecting mental maneuvers. Every time we justify ourselves, defensiveness is at work. Whenever we insist on our own rightness, force others to see something our way, or try to control what happens, defensiveness is present. We need great honesty and humility to unmask ourselves, to see the self-protective motives that keep us from more appropriate ones.

Right Understanding

Right understanding means clear-seeing, seeing reality as it truly is, without the blinders of desires, aversions, or delusions. It is seeing the truth of things unclouded by any smoke screens that self-sense throws up to protect itself. Life itself teaches us these truths at one level, just as we may intellectually comprehend them even more superficially. Faithful and careful awareness practice brings increasingly deeper, clearer seeing — the kind of seeing that can radically purify the heart.

Early insight.   What is called the early "insight knowledges" comes from deepening meditation practice. This is not conceptual knowledge or even simple lived awareness of unsatisfactoriness, impermanence, and emptiness. In meditation, understanding comes by direct seeing, which produces life-changing learning.

The first insight knowledge is of mental and physical reality. It means clearly understanding physical realities, such as sensations we call painful or the sound when a bell is struck. It also means understanding mental phenomena — consciousness and mind-states; for example, just what is a thought, or what is anger or fear? We also clearly distinguish physical from mental phenomena.

A second insight knowledge is cause and effect. We see how pleasantness of feeling-tone easily leads to greed if we are not alert, how unpleasantness draws out aversion, and how we become bored and inattentive when feeling-tone is neutral. Clear awareness of feeling-tone can keep us from moving into greed, aversion, or delusion.

We also see how intentions precede each action. Awareness of intention lets us cancel it when not appropriate. If we fail to see intentions, they impel unskillful action whenever an unwholesome mind-state gets strong. Feeling-tone and intention mark crucial points of freedom once we clearly see cause and effect regarding them.

Knowledge of cause and effect goes even deeper. We see multiple cause-effect relationships in our choices, how they condition future options and situations. We realize that each choice to indulge a habit, obsession, compulsion, or addiction tilts the balance, making it easier to so choose the next time. We see how each "no" to unwholesomeness makes saying "no" again easier. We realize that nothing is free; everything counts, has its consequences.

We see the absolute interconnection of all of us in and with all of nature! Insight practice shows how our choices affect not only ourselves and all beings, but all matter also. As a people, we are just becoming aware of how habits of waste affect our environment. In practice, we see even more subtle connections that attest to everything's being part of one cosmic process. We become attentive to the effects of all our choices. We see these truths by faithfully paying full attention to physical and mental experiences that draw awareness to themselves.

The three characteristics. Another insight knowledge reveals the nature of conditioned reality, of realities subject to cause and effect. A rugged period of practice teaches us to see clearly the three characteristics that mark everything except *nibbana.*

We see for ourselves the truth of suffering in all lives. Irrefutable meditation experiences show the fleeting nature of phenomena, how things come into existence simply to pass out again. We comprehend what the Buddha meant by no-self, understanding how — since only *nibbana* is unchanging — all lived realities are truly only processes with a beginning and end.

This stage of practice is often very unpleasant; however, it purges attachments, develops patience and compassion, and finally leads to a holy life. These insights leave us greatly humbled and deeply committed to spiritual practice. Meditation becomes "automatic," with sharp, clear, and penetrating understanding.

Knowing the path. The practice next settles into a delightfully easy period with the danger of attachment to pleasant meditation experience. Eventually, deepening knowledge brings the sure seeing of the right path of practice. We realize that we do not practice for comfort or pleasure, but for purification. We understand that purifying conduct and mind is the only way out of the human dilemma, that no magic or hard wishing or other maneuver does the job. This greatly lessens attachment to pleasantness and prepares us for the even more rugged purgation that follows.

Advanced insight. In advanced insight, we radically experience the three characteristics. We see clearly what physics has confirmed — that the very solid-looking objects of experience only look solid. They are mostly space filled with millions of whirling atoms. All is change; even consciousness itself dies with each experience and is reborn with the next.

We deeply realize that what is never stationery, never lasting, can never be lastingly satisfying. The suffering in even pleasant experience becomes very apparent. All pleasures end; all favorite cups eventually break. All relationships come to parting — by death, if not before. However beautiful, delightful, inspiring, or joy-filled an experience, it ends and therefore brings no lasting satisfaction.

We clearly see that nothing has any unchanging fixedness we can consider a permanent, enduring entity. We recognize how what we call ourselves are simply interlocking processes that have come together because of conditions and will eventually come apart. All is process, the constant interchange of processes within processes within processes. Often these realizations come with stark feelings of aloneness, impotence, vulnerability, and lack. The purgation is rigorous and intense.

A great yearning for liberation that consumes all of one's being eventually comes. Next follows the deeply balanced equanimity of complete surrender; we accept any and all occurrences equally. This balanced state of mind is "near" *nibbana.*

Fruition. Advanced insight culminates in "touching" *nibbana,* being "in" the one Reality not subject to the fluctuations, insecurity, and suffering of human life. *Nibbana* — the unconditioned, the unchanging, the unborn, the undying, the permanent, peace, rest, haven, home — is beyond any earthly joy, delight, or stillness. Thing-ness and flux cease; faith has been perfected, and we now know by direct experience.

Right Motivation

Once we have seen clearly, have come to wisdom or spiritual fruition, it affects how we live in the world. There are three traditional right motives or intentions: renunciation, loving-kindness, and compassionate non-violence. These counter greed, self-centeredness, and cruelty.

Renunciation. Renunciation is not suppression or heavy-handed self-control, but a willing letting-go. Understanding that we must relinquish what is harmful is easy, needing only simple common sense. Precepts help by giving us guidelines.

Next we let go of things that easily lead to harming. Buddhist monastics take additional precepts for this. They fast from midday until dawn, give up frivolous entertainment, and refrain from adorning their persons. They avoid unnecessary ease of posture, and some do not handle money.

A third level of renunciation — refraining from things that draw attention from what is important — is very difficult. In meditation practice, we give up thinking, looking around, and unnecessary activity that disturbs concentration. In daily life, we must ruthlessly surrender whatever distracts us from our spiritual purpose.

The final relinquishment — of separate self-sense and the suffering that goes with it — is the fruit of spiritual practice. When we deeply understand suffering, impermanence, no-self, and the effects of actions, we want this final relinquishment. We cannot *make* the transforming touch of *nibbana* or God happen, but we can prepare for it. We can live according to the eightfold noble path: being moral, purifying mental contents, and cultivating wisdom and radical purity of heart.

Loving-kindness and harmlessness. We have already discussed loving-kindness, the second correct motivation. It must not be only a nice feeling to enjoy, but must translate into action. Harmonious behavior and attitudes support loving-kindness. Looking for good in others makes loving-kindness habitual.

The third right mind-set, harmlessness and compassion, flows from loving-kindness and from understanding suffering and the effects of choices. As spiritual practice ripens, so does compassion. Practicing renunciation and mindfulness in daily life helps develop it. We shrink from inflicting hurt, and feel great compassion for those who do harm, knowing they are making themselves great suffering. Wisdom and compassion, the two great wings of Buddhism, mutually feed each other.

One beautiful example is that of a British hostage released in 1990. When asked if he wanted revenge, he said no, for he would not maim himself with such motives. In contrast, an American hostage released in 1991 felt his captors should be chained for twenty years, the cumulative amount of time he and fellow captives were chained. Which hostage is now truly free?

Virtues. Buddhist teachings list ten virtues that the Buddha perfected and that each spiritual practitioner must develop. They make right intention more concrete for us.

First is generosity, exactly the opposite of clinging or grasping, a major cause of suffering. Open-handedness toward others celebrates our very real oneness, and bends us to meeting others' needs as if they were our own. The Buddha considered this a cardinal practice.

We have already discussed the next four. Morality is the necessary basis for further purification, and renunciation is the deepening, progressive letting-go that constitutes spiritual work. Wisdom, fully right understanding, finally liberates us. Effort appears in more Buddhist lists of necessary qualities than any other.

Sixth is patience. We must be willing to be worked on, accept purgation without complaint in both meditation practice and life. Truthfulness, the seventh, goes beyond not lying; our whole being is to *become* truth. This means being fully in accord with reality, part of which is necessary self-knowledge.

Eighth is resolution. If we do not stick with spiritual work when it is not to our liking, we will not move very far. We must be constant in times of difficulty as well as delight. People have asked if they should postpone daily sitting when they cannot "get with it." This temptation is dangerous; if we practice only when we feel like it, we avoid necessary corrective experiences.

The ninth virtue of loving-kindness is the foundational heavenly mind-state; it carries within it compassion and sympathetic joy. The tenth virtue is equanimity, fourth of the heavenly mind-states. With equanimity, we stay surrendered; we remain balanced within the fluctuating tides of fortune in our own and others' lives.

In these virtues, our "touching" *nibbana* becomes a consecrated life. May we all work with diligence to know the Ultimate Reality and live a life showing the fruits of this knowing.

M.J.M.

Chapter 20

ST. JOHN AND THE BUDDHA ON PURIFICATION FOR FRUITION AND TRANSFORMATION
Integrative Summary

The earlier chapters of Part III discussed the purification of conduct and of mental contents. In these chapters, both John of the Cross and the Buddha agree that spiritual practice demands serious and concrete discipline. They teach us specific ways to purify ourselves in mind and body. They strongly emphasize self-emptying in the transformation process. However, in the last two chapters of this section, "Contemplative Purification" and "Purification of the Heart," both John and the Buddha teach that purification of the heart ultimately lies beyond our human capacity. It is gift. We need a "higher power" to heal and transform our wounded hearts.

The Deep Need for Healing

To begin with, both John and the Buddha are profoundly aware of the extent of our sinfulness and brokenness. For John of the Cross, the pleasure principle has sunk its roots deep within us. It unconsciously and pervasively motivates much of what we do, even our most religious actions. It appears in such forms as spiritual pride, avarice, lust, gluttony, envy, anger, and sloth. It disguises itself in consoling prayer experiences to which we become attached, or in acts of service to others fueled by unrecognized needs for acceptance and approval.

The Buddha was also aware of strongly conditioned tendencies of the heart. They manifest themselves when we tenaciously cling to our opinions, ideas, and theories, and remain closed to other ways of thinking. Subtle forms of selfishness reveal themselves in self-defensive behavior, unconscious assumptions, and the lust for power, prestige, and ambition.

Because the roots of sinfulness and conditioning lie so deeply hidden within us, we are powerless to heal and purify ourselves. Both John and the Buddha agree that we need something beyond human effort to illumine our wounded self-love and to transform us.

The Healing Power of Awareness

According to John of the Cross, contemplation enlightens the darkness of our hearts and heals the hidden roots of our inability to love as God created us to love. In contemplation, which John defines as infused loving wisdom of God, God illumines us and purges, heals, and transforms all that obstructs our union with God through love.

Contemplative purification is a deepening process that calls for passivity and surrender to God's Spirit. There are periods of emotional highs and lows. There are times of searing, painful self-knowledge followed by deeper peace and interior freedom. Moments of consolation may follow days or months of dryness and interior darkness. But throughout all the peaks and valleys of the transformative process, we must remain passive, receptive, and open to all that God desires to accomplish within us. We must persevere in prayer and embrace all that God sends us in faith, hope, and love.

For the Buddha, it is wisdom, the fruit of right understanding, that sheds light upon the dark forces of our minds and transforms our hearts. Clear seeing comes from sustained, formal awareness practice and sincere spiritual living every day. This gradually bestows deeper and sharper insight into the truth of our lives and the nature of reality. Right understanding, however, involves more than just meditative insight into our interior poverty and the nature of reality; clear seeing truly purifies us and uproots the strongly conditioned tendencies of the mind and heart.

This path of purification is a dynamic process that requires sustained passivity, surrender, and openness. As insight deepens we begin to understand the nature of physical and mental reality. We gain insight into how we push away the unpleasant in our lives and cling tenaciously to the pleasant. We become acutely aware of our underlying intentions and motivations and see how our daily choices affect ourselves and others. We perceive the truth of suffering, the unsatisfactoriness of life, and the fleeting nature of phenomena. Such realizations often come with stark feelings of highs and lows, aloneness, vulnerability, and impotence. There are periods of joy, happiness, and freedom as well as struggle, suffering, and feelings of oppression. But throughout all the stages of deepening insight, a profound transformation takes place to which we must remain open and surrendered in faith and trust.

Transformation: The Fruit of Purification

Both the Buddha and John of the Cross believe that the fruits of purification make the spiritual journey worthwhile. John writes of the freedom experienced when we arrive at union with God through love. Liberated from our enslavement to disordered desires and the pleasure principle, we can freely respond to the movement of the Holy Spirit in our lives. Just as fire transforms a log of wood so that the wood possesses the properties and actions of fire, God transforms us so that we share the very properties and actions of God. Love becomes the unifying factor of our lives. In short, we love God, others, and the world with the unconditional, compassionate, and merciful love of God.

Similarly, the Buddha teaches that the wisdom born from right understanding profoundly affects how we live in this world. If we closely examine the state of right motivation, what emerges is the description of a person totally dedicated to love. The motives of renunciation, loving-kindness, and non-violence depict a life completely committed to the ideals of love and compassion. Renunciation calls for letting go of harming and self-centeredness so we can love more freely and purely. Loving-kindness, harmlessness, and compassionate non-violence speak for themselves. They require harmonious and caring behavior and a willingness to forgive even in the most painful, evil, and unjust situations. Truly, to live in such a way is to touch *nibbana* — a state of peace, rest, and tranquility — even in the midst of suffering.

The Importance of Spiritual Practice

The doctrines of John of the Cross and the Buddha on contemplative purification of the heart point once more to the importance of serious meditation practice. We all experience the need for radical purification and our helplessness in healing ourselves. John and the Buddha proclaim a message of hope to all who long for deeper liberation and transformation. They challenge us to surrender ourselves to God, to the *Dhamma,* through a life of serious prayer and committed spiritual living.

Insight meditation is a path of purification. It develops clear insight into the true nature of life, especially our wounded self-love. It gives us the freedom that is born of clear seeing. Furthermore, moment-to-moment awareness, being simply with what is in the present moment, teaches us how to remain open, passive, and surrendered to the purifying process. If practiced seriously with an attitude of faith and love, trusting in the merciful love of God, it will bring about the healing and wholeness for which we long and for which God created us.

D.C.

Part IV

Questions
Christians Ask

Chapter 21

ON PRAYER, MEDITATION, AND CONTEMPLATION

The preceding chapters of this book present the history, practice, and theory of Christian insight meditation. In this last part we address questions frequently raised about the practice during our retreats.

No Set Terminology

We are often asked, for example, to define prayer, meditation, and contemplation and to describe the relationship between them. Unfortunately, we cannot give a definitive answer to this question. These words are used so differently both within and across traditions that one common set of definitions for everybody is impossible.

Some prefer to use the word "prayer" only when describing communion with a personal God within a religious tradition. They limit the term "meditation" to spiritual practice before the Absolute or Unconditioned, but without reference to religion. In this understanding, prayer assumes faith in a personal God, whereas meditation does not.

Also, different traditions use the same word to refer to different practices. Christians frequently think of meditation as discursive or step-by-step mental prayer; for Buddhists, meditation is a non-discursive practice that emphasizes relinquishing voluntary thought, imagination, memory, and emotion to pay close attention to immediate experience.

Even within the same religious tradition, spiritual masters use the same word in different ways. In his *Spiritual Exercises,* Ignatius of Loyola presents contemplation as imaginative reflection on scenes from the Gospel to arouse fervor for commitment to Jesus, whereas John of the Cross, a fellow Spaniard living in the same century as Ignatius, thinks of contemplation as an inflow of God into the soul.[1]

To avoid confusion, we try to state clearly our understanding of these terms when we use them in the context of Christian insight meditation. We do so, not to imply that ours is the preferred understanding, but only to situate insight meditation in the Christian prayer life.

Prayer

Prayer is the general category in which meditation and contemplation are specific types. Prayer is essentially personal communion with God in faith, hope, and love. At the risk of oversimplification, we can say that this communion may be exterior or interior depending on which aspect of the human person it expresses. Exterior prayer refers to those social, communal, externally expressive forms of communion with God. These include Eucharist, sacraments and liturgical worship, sacred ritual, religious song and dance, popular devotions like the public recitation of the rosary or stations of the cross, pilgrimages and other external ways of praising, thanking, adoring, and petitioning God.

By contrast, interior prayer (or mental prayer, as it is often called) takes place primarily within our mind and heart. Here we enter privately into the sanctuary of our own being to be alone with the Alone present within us. Traditionally, meditation and contemplation are ways of interior prayer. Among Carmelites, meditation usually means all that we do to establish communion with God in interior prayer, whereas contemplation is what God does in us, the inflow of divine loving knowledge into our beings.

Meditation

Meditation can be either discursive or non-discursive. Discursive meditation involves thinking, reasoning, imagining, remembering, and feeling as we described earlier in chapter 18. John of the Cross calls this discursive process meditation; St. Ignatius of Loyola calls it contemplation when he invites us to reflect prayerfully on the mystery of Jesus' Incarnation.

Non-discursive meditation, on the other hand, attempts to quiet these mental activities in order to be silent and passive before God, receptive to whatever God chooses to communicate to us. The Eastern traditions generally consider meditation as a non-discursive process.

Non-discursive meditation usually involves four basic elements: a suitable place, a proper posture, a mental device or object of focus — a sacred word or phrase, a mantra, an icon, the breath — and a passive attitude.[2] Non-discursive meditation may also emphasize either concentration or awareness, depending on whether the object of focus is one chosen thing or the total experiencing of the organism. The difference between concentrative and awareness meditation will be explained further in chapter 24.

Contemplation

Following St. John of the Cross, we use the word "contemplation" to refer only to God's direct self-communication to a person disposed through self-emptying in faith and love to receive this intimate revelation. It is not our activity, but God's. It is not our achievement, but a grace freely given to us. It is not something we do to ourselves; rather, it is something God does in us. We dispose ourselves in meditation to receive this grace, but ultimately contemplation is God's free gift to us.

In contemplation, God "fires the soul in the spirit of love" (N1, 10, 6) and "supernaturally instructs [it] in ... divine wisdom" (N1, 12, 4). Contemplation "is knowledge and love together, that is, loving knowledge" (F3, 32). Contemplation shares in God's own loving knowledge that purifies and transforms our human knowing and loving so that we know and love as God knows and loves. We receive this contemplation by opening ourselves to it, just as we receive sunlight into a room when we open the shutters on the window. It is God's loving knowledge communicated to us in contemplation that transforms us and unites us with God in love.

Christian Insight Meditation

Within this conceptual framework, Christian insight meditation is a method of non-discursive meditation. This practice helps dispose us for the gift of contemplation by actively purifying our sense and spirit through faith, hope, and love.

It is particularly valuable for those whom God leads beyond the beginning stages of discursive prayer and begins to place in the state of contemplation. The practice helps them maintain the non-discursive, passive, surrendered, loving attention in God's presence that John recommends for those who are beyond the stage of beginners. By simply watching the breath and gently noting all that comes into awareness, neither consciously pushing away nor clinging to any arising phenomenon, we let go of discursive prayer.

Moreover, readiness to accept passively everything that comes into consciousness disposes us to receive in awareness all the unresolved conflicts, hurts, and grief hidden in our unconscious. Previously, our efforts to sustain and to derive satisfaction from discursive reflection prevented these phenomena from becoming conscious; now this self-knowledge is received passively in awareness, like a painful but loving gift of God, to be clearly seen, felt, and healed.

The experience of silence and solitude that comes with faithful insight practice also strengthens our longing for God and our desire to hear God's Word awakening, as if from sleep, in the depths of our being. This attitude of loving attention to God grows, not only during formal mental prayer, but throughout the entire day. It heightens our readiness to perceive God communicating with us through all creation and in all the events of our daily life.

Finally, in insight meditation we see sensations, thoughts, emotions, moods, feelings, pain, terror, and delight come into consciousness; these are noted and then pass out of consciousness. Observing closely this constant flow of phenomena deepens our appreciation of the truth expressed in the famous Bookmark of St. Teresa: "All things pass away...God alone suffices."

Mental Noting
and Contemplative Prayer

The soft mental noting that is characteristic of Christian insight meditation fosters the interior non-attachment we need for contemplative prayer to develop. At times, we experience profound joy and love for God. Noting these experiences maintains sharp, clear awareness and keeps us from getting lost in these delightful moments. We enjoy them as long as they last, but let go of them when they pass. Noting also enables us to be present to mental and physical pain, aware of its passing nature, and not be overcome by it or turn away from it simply because it is unpleasant.

At times, our absorption in God can be so deep and powerful that we are unable to continue the mental noting. We seem completely surrendered to God and open to all that God chooses to do in us. We feel deeply touched by God, if only for a short time. We feel powerless to do anything for as long as this touch lasts. But when it passes, we resume noting our experiencing. We trust that God's own purpose has been accomplished in this ineffable moment and continue in the non-attached attitude that is essential for progress in contemplative prayer.

Non-Discursive Meditation
as Contemplative Prayer

We said above that contemplation is God's work, not our own. Nonetheless, we can call non-discursive meditation contemplative prayer. Its non-discursive quality and passive attitude help dispose us to receive the communication of God's loving knowledge. So we call Christian insight meditation contemplative prayer, just as we speak of centering prayer, the Jesus prayer, praying with icons, *lectio divina,* and Christian meditation as contemplative prayer.

Indeed, there are many ways of praying contemplatively. When teaching her nuns to pray, St. Teresa of Jesus reminded them of the old sister who became a great contemplative through faithfully praying her Our Fathers every day. However, the specific quality of Christian insight meditation as contemplative prayer is its focus on purifying the heart and emptying out self to dispose us to receive God's gift of contemplation.

Insight Meditation for Beginners

We are frequently asked whether beginners in interior prayer may safely begin immediately with non-discursive meditation. Can they dispense with the classic Christian model of starting with discursive meditation and then gradually moving to non-discursive or contemplative prayer when the signs indicate that it is time to do so?

John of the Cross counsels discursive meditation for beginners to deepen their knowledge and love of Jesus Christ. The delight they discover in this new knowledge and love reinforces their commitment to follow Christ, especially in hard times. John maintains that leaving discursive meditation before this knowledge and love is established in their souls can be as detrimental as continuing discursive meditation when God clearly is leading them into contemplation.

By contrast, the Buddhist tradition ordinarily does not

use discursive meditation. Beginners start with a stable posture, a suitable place, an object of focus, and a passive attitude. The meditation practice then unfolds through the normal developmental stages that lead eventually to enlightenment. Similarly, many Christians report never being able to pray discursively; from the very beginning of their spiritual journey they have practiced some form of non-discursive meditation. As their meditation has deepened, their knowledge and love of God has also grown.

We maintain that Christians can begin interior prayer with non-discursive meditation, provided their knowledge and love of God is being nourished through other sources, such as liturgical worship, *lectio divina,* and spiritual reading. When knowledge and love of God deepen through other sources, insisting on discursive meditation is not necessary. Also, simply doing the meditation practice, making oneself fully open to God's purifying action, is itself a continuing act of love for God.

Nevertheless, persons who undertake the spiritual journey must be guided according to their own individual needs. Some may indeed be drawn to discursive meditation in the beginning and profit from it greatly. Yet eventually even they must be helped to let go of it when God calls them to a deeper, more contemplative way of praying.

K.C.

Chapter 22

ON JESUS CHRIST AND THE HOLY SPIRIT

The questions most often asked about Christian insight meditation concern Jesus Christ and the Holy Spirit. During insight meditation we do not think about Jesus, nor imagine him, nor repeat his sacred name, nor gaze upon the crucifix or a sacred icon. We simply sit quietly, anchored in the breath, open to observe peacefully whatever comes into our awareness, neither avoiding nor clinging to anything. Where is Jesus Christ in this? Since we have other forms of Christian contemplative prayer that specifically focus on Jesus by name or word or image, why would we choose a method that does not? Does watching the breath and other experiences of body and mind really open us to the guidance of the Holy Spirit?

The Imitation of Christ

Like other methods of contemplative prayer, Jesus is central to Christian insight meditation. However, we relate to Christ in this practice primarily by imitating in it his death on the cross. Our self-emptying during meditation is our loving response to him who emptied himself on the cross for love of us.

The principal experience of Jesus that interests us in insight meditation is his death on the cross and his resurrection from the dead. We attempt to enter this experience by cultivating non-attachment, not only to objects in the world around us that delight us, but especially to the desires, thoughts, memories, feelings, and emotions of our own inner world. Through non-attachment we die to the unreal self created over our lifetime by disordered desires, thoughts, imagination, and emotions and rise to a new life in Christ who is hidden in the very substance of our soul.

Jesus demands death to this unreal self for Christian discipleship. "Those who want to follow me must renounce themselves, take up their cross and follow me. Those who want to save their life must lose it; those who lose their life for my sake, and for the sake of the Gospel, save it. What gain is it to win the whole world and ruin one's life? And indeed, what can one offer in exchange for one's life?" (Mk 8:34–38). In meditation we deliberately stop giving psychic energy to all desires, thoughts, feelings, memories, images, and emotions that lead us away from Christ's death and prevent his rising in our lives.

St. Paul

With St. Paul we try to imitate Christ who "emptied himself," yet reigns in glory (Ph 2:5ff). This imitation demands not merely recalling Christ's death, but actually sharing it: "All I want," Paul told the Philippians, "is to know Christ and the power of his resurrection and to share his suffering by reproducing the pattern of his death. That is the way I can hope to take my place in the resurrection of the dead" (Ph 3:10–11). In this spirit, Christian insight meditation pays careful attention not only to delightful interior experiences, but equally so to pain and suffering, realizing the call to unsuspected new life contained in them.

St. John of the Cross

As we saw earlier in Part III, St. John of the Cross teaches that imitating Christ is the essential practice for purifying our hearts and preparing them for God's transforming love in contemplation. For John, imitating Christ means primarily imitating his "living death of the cross, sensory and spiritual, exterior and interior" (A2, 7, 11). He observes: "Some are content with a certain degree of virtue, perseverance in prayer, and mortification, but never achieve the nakedness, poverty, selflessness, or spiritual purity (which are all the same) about which the Lord counsels us [in Mark 8:34–35]" (A2, 7, 5).

Furthermore, imitating Jesus' death is not limited to beginners in prayer who struggle to overcome disordered sensory appetites; it is required for the entire journey to union with and transformation in God. "Nothing, nothing, nothing,..." John writes on the middle road of his Sketch of Mt. Carmel, "and even on the Mount nothing."[1] The "truly devout," John explains, "seek the living image of Christ crucified within themselves, and thereby they are pleased rather to have everything taken from them and to be left with nothing" (A3, 35, 5).

There is never a moment in the spiritual journey when Jesus' total self-emptying on the cross ceases to be the model for Christians who desire union with God in love. Thus, no matter where we are along the journey, we sit in meditation before God with clear, sharp, non-attached awareness. We trust that, as we strive to let go of every disordered sensory and spiritual attachment, we are at the very same time becoming transformed in Divine Wisdom, the Son of God, for, as John assures us, "there can be no void in nature" (A2, 15, 4).

Paschal Mystery

By imitating Jesus' "living death on the cross," we attempt in Christian insight meditation to enter completely into the paschal mystery — the death and resurrection of Jesus Christ. This, Vatican II taught us, is the heart of Christian life, worship, and spirituality. We thereby prepare to proclaim in Eucharist the "Mystery of our Faith — Christ has died, Christ has risen, Christ will come again!"

These words both affirm our faith in the Lord of History and commit us to embrace the dying and rising involved in each day's struggle to free ourselves from everything that keeps us from giving our lives in love and service to others. "The Son of Man came, not to be served, but to serve and to give his life for as a ransom for many" (Mk 10:45).

Devotion to the Holy Spirit

Jesus' death on the cross brought the outpouring of his Spirit. "One of the soldiers pierced his side with a lance"; observes an eyewitness, "and immediately there came out blood and water" (Jn 19:34–35). In Christian insight meditation, imitating Jesus' total self-emptying on the cross opens our hearts to receive this outpouring of his Spirit into our lives.

Following his resurrection, Jesus "breathed" on his disciples and said "Receive the Holy Spirit" (Jn 20:22). From its very beginnings, Christianity has attached deep spiritual significance to the breath. Our breathing reminds us that God breathed life into us at our creation and constantly sustains us by empowering us to breathe; it recalls especially the outpouring of Jesus' Spirit to renew our lives.

Because of its profound biblical symbolism, Christians have quite naturally incorporated the breath into their prayer. Eastern Christianity's "Jesus Prayer" coordinates the constant repetition of "Lord Jesus Christ, Son of the Living God, have mercy on me, a sinner" with each inhalation and exhalation. John of the Cross, too, in the final words of *The Living Flame of Love,* describes the breathing of a person united and transformed in God as filled "with good and glory in which [the Holy Spirit] enkindled it in love of himself, indescribably and incomprehensibly, in the depths of God" (F4, 17).

In Christian insight meditation, sitting quietly with our breathing has sacred significance. It deepens awareness of our "substantial union" with God and our longing for the "union of likeness" in which we are transformed in God through love (A2, 5, 3). It anchors our attention during prayer, symbolizes our openness to receive the Holy Spirit, and, most importantly, aims to bring out all our motivation under the Spirit's guidance.

Transformation of Motivation

St. John of the Cross holds that the main psychological fruit of transformation in God through contemplation is motivational. When we are united with God in perfect love, we are no longer moved to seek satisfaction from sensory and spiritual objects as we were in early stages of the spiritual journey; rather, we are moved only by the Holy Spirit. Citing Mary of Nazareth as an example of this, John says of her: "Raised from the beginning to this high state, she never had the form of any creature impressed on her soul, nor was she moved by any, for she was always moved by the Holy Spirit" (A3, 2, 10).

To dispose ourselves to be "always moved by the Holy Spirit," John counsels us to consciously direct our activities to God in their very first movements. For example, as soon as we feel ourselves moved to satisfy ourselves in some object, John advises us to lift that movement to God. The more aware we become of our first movements toward action, the more free we are to direct these actions toward God's honor and glory. This increasing awareness and freedom prepares us to be moved in all our actions by the Holy Spirit.

Awareness of First Movements

In this transformation process, insight meditation helps us to become increasingly aware of our first movements. Frequently, we act unaware of the interior movements that lead to our external behavior. In the years when I smoked a pack of cigarettes a day, I was often amazed at how frequently I became aware that I was smoking only as I was snuffing out my cigarette in an ashtray.

At those times I was completely unaware of the first impulse to light up, the movement of my hand for the pack in my shirt pocket, striking the match, the first deep inhaling of smoke, and flicking the ashes in the ash trays (and more often on the floor). A whole chain of movements had taken place before I became aware that I was smoking. Without this awareness, I was not free to intervene at some point in this series of events and choose not to smoke.

As we attend in meditation to all that we experience — body sensations, thoughts, memories, feelings, emotions, desires, intentions — we gradually become aware of the first movements that eventually lead us to action. We recognize, for example, a feeling of pleasantness or unpleasantness or neutrality associated with the memory of a particular person. A pleasant feeling draws out of us a mind-state such as delight or longing; fear or anger arises from an unpleasant feeling; boredom or indifference comes from a neutral feeling.

Out of such mind-states an intention forms to perform an action. Angered by the unpleasant feeling associated with the memory of a painful encounter with some person in the past, we begin planning an act of retaliation for the next time we see the person. As we become aware of and note this chain of events within ourselves, we begin to experience freedom.

We gradually recognize that the feeling of unpleasantness at the memory of this person need not lead to indulging anger. We can choose to react with compassion. Or anger over past events need not move us to act negatively in our next meeting. We can choose to act cooperatively and compassionately.

The more aware we are of all these interior movements, the more freedom we have to choose appropriate responses to the persons and events of our lives. We can act more intentionally and less compulsively. Our behavior becomes more proactive and less reactive.

Mindfulness and awareness, not only in formal prayer, but in the many activities and interpersonal interactions throughout the day, give us greater freedom to raise the first movements of our minds and hearts to God and direct our behavior to God's honor and glory. This mindfulness disposes us to be moved more by the Holy Spirit than by our own unrecognized impulses, feelings, and emotions. We taste more often the fruits of the Spirit — love, joy, peace, patience, kindness, goodness, trustfulness, gentleness, and self-control (Ga 5:22).

Summary

Christian insight meditation, then, involves imitating Jesus' self-emptying on the cross and disposing ourselves to be moved in all that we do by the Holy Spirit. If after years of practicing insight meditation, we continue trying to control the outcome of all that happens in our lives, close our hearts to our neighbors, fear failure, and cannot manage our selfish impulses, we recognize that our heart is still far from pure and that our transformation is going to take some time.

This awareness does not cause us guilt or discouragement. It only helps us realize how strongly we resist transformation and how deeply rooted are the effects of original sin in our soul. We become more aware of our absolute need for God's love to heal and transform us. Such understanding is a common fruit of Christian insight practice. Like every method of Christian prayer, we evaluate it by its fruits.

K.C.

Chapter 23

ON CHURCH TEACHINGS

Is Christian insight meditation sanctioned by the Catholic Church? Does not Cardinal Ratzinger's October 15, 1989, "Letter to Bishops of the Catholic Church on Some Aspects of Christian Meditation" specifically warn us against praying according to this method? If these Eastern meditation practices are so helpful to Christian prayer, why have American Catholics been taught so little about them? Why have we been taught so little about our own Christian traditions of meditation and contemplation?

Church Teaching

We group questions like these, which come up in our retreats, under the heading of Church teaching. As already noted in the Preface, the Second Vatican Council articulated the official Roman Catholic respect for the ancient religions of the East and their spiritual practices. This position encourages Catholic religious missionaries to assimilate their ascetical and contemplative practices that reveal God's hand at work in ancient cultures before the coming of Gospel (*Nostra Aetate,* no. 2; *Ad Gentes,* no. 18).

Implementing the Council's commitment to interfaith dialogue, Pope Paul VI established the Secretariat for Non-Christian Religions, later renamed the Council for Interreligious Dialogue. He entrusted to the Benedictines and Cistercians the responsibility for dialogue with monks of Asian religions. They responded enthusiastically, leading eventually to the formation in the United States of the North American Board for East-West Dialogue.

The Bangkok monastic conference in 1968, where Thomas Merton died, resulted from Paul VI's initiative. Today, interreligious dialogue includes scholarly discussion, shared prayer, exchange of monastic hospitality, and combined compassionate social action.

Pope John Paul II has continued to promote interfaith collaboration. During his pontificate, the work of the Council for Interreligious Dialog has increased. On pilgrimage to Asia in 1981, the Pope stated: "The Church of Jesus Christ in this age experiences a profound need to enter into contact and dialogue with [Hinduism, Buddhism, and Islam]...so that mutual understanding and collaboration may grow; so that moral values may be strengthened; so that God may be praised in creation."[1]

Christian Insight Meditation

The Vatican II documents and the Benedictines' example have guided our efforts to assimilate Theravadan Buddhism's *vipassana* (insight) meditation into the Christian contemplative tradition. But why attempt this assimilation in the first place?

To cite just one benefit, insight meditation enhances John of the Cross's teaching on self-emptying. He explains, for example, that emptying sense and spirit disposes us for God's transforming love in contemplation. However, John provides little concrete methodology for practicing and maintaining this emptiness within prayer.

Insight meditation also emphasizes self-emptying as a condition for the emergence of wisdom and compassion. It, however, provides a detailed meditation methodology for doing this. Assimilating the insight method of self-emptying into Christian contemplative prayer thus helps Christians who embrace John's teaching that "evangelical perfection...lies in nakedness and emptiness of sense and spirit" (F3, 47) and who desire to dispose themselves through self-emptying for God's purifying and unifying love in contemplation.

1989 Vatican Letter

In 1989, the Vatican Congregation for the Doctrine of the Faith issued its "Letter to the Bishops of the Catholic Church on Some Aspects of Christian Meditation."[2] Probably not coincidentally, the letter was signed by Cardinal Ratzinger on October 15, the feast of St. Teresa of Avila, and released December 14, the feast of St. John of the Cross. Perhaps this quietly recommends these two Carmelite Doctors of the Church in the field of spirituality as teachers of authentic Christian meditation.

The letter reaffirms Vatican II's recognition of the value of Eastern spiritual practices for Christian prayer. However, it warns of possible dangers in the process of assimilating these practices, such as overabsorption in self or disregard for Jesus as the "Way" to divine union. The letter affirms, as we do in retreats, that union with God is primarily a union of wills, a union of likeness in which "God's will and the soul's are in conformity, so that nothing in the one is repugnant to the other" (A2, 5, 3).

Also, it advocates, as we do, a Christian understanding of self-emptying. Thus, non-attachment to desires, sensations, thoughts, images, memories, and emotions is not an end in itself; rather, it is a necessary discipline to free us from the interior obstacles created by attachments to these phenomena that prevent us from giving ourselves totally to God and others in love and service.

Christian insight meditation directly addresses the major concerns of the Vatican's warning. For example, the letter cautions against misinterpreting meditation experiences. It expresses concern about Christians using Eastern methods "to generate spiritual experiences similar to those described in the writings of certain Christian mystics" (no. 12) or who take "a feeling of quiet and relaxation, pleasing sensations, perhaps even phenomena of light or warmth...for the authentic consolations of the Holy Spirit" (no. 28). Drawing on the Gospel, Theravadan Buddhism, and John of the Cross, we emphasize not pleasant or extraordinary experiences, but interior purification.

With John of the Cross, we explain that "one act done in charity is more precious in God's sight than all the visions and [extraordinary] communications possible" (A2, 22, 19). We hold with Joseph Goldstein, a leading American teacher of insight meditation, that "pleasant or painful feelings do not indicate how well your practice is going. The goals we seek through practice are wisdom and compassion, not some permanent tingle."[3] Following Jesus, we insist that purifying the heart is absolutely necessary for seeing God.

Pope John Paul II perhaps best summarizes the Church's position on using Eastern meditation practices in Christian prayer. In a 1982 homily honoring St. Teresa of Avila and footnoted in the Vatican's letter, the Pontiff states: "Any method of prayer is valid insofar as it is inspired by Christ and leads to Christ, who is the way, the truth, and the life."[4] It is not the method *per se* that determines its validity for Christians, but the faith and love of the person using the method.

Thus, Christians can use insight meditation practice to deepen their personal union with God in love, to enter more fully into Jesus' paschal mystery, and to open themselves completely to the inspirations of the Holy Spirit. This transforms Theravadan Buddhist *vipassana* into Christian insight meditation.

Education for Contemplation

Why has the Church in the United States not taught meditation and contemplative prayer as part of its normal religious education? This question, asked frequently by angry and disappointed Catholics who feel cheated of a precious birthright, probably has many answers.

One explanation is the relative youth of the American Church and its history as an immigrant community. Since the establishment of the American hierarchy a little over two hundred years ago when John Carroll was appointed first bishop of Baltimore, the hierarchy's principal concern has been to maintain the Church as a visible Christian presence in the United States.

Associated with this was the purpose of educating millions of Catholic immigrants from Europe. They were taught the basics of Christian doctrine to sustain their faith in the new world and were given a human education necessary to take their place in American society. In this agenda, there was little room for contemplative prayer.

By the middle of this century, however, the Church was quite well established in American society and its members well educated and positioned. Catholics now began to long for a deeper experience of Christian faith. Probably more than any other single person, Thomas Merton awakened the American Church to a desire for a contemplative Christianity. Today, judging from the sheer volume of literature and programs in spirituality, this desire has become a widespread thirst in the American Church.

In his May 1993 "Ad Limina" address to the bishops of Iowa, Kansas, Missouri, and Nebraska, Pope John Paul II pointed to this thirst as a major pastoral challenge for the Church in the United States today. "In the midst of [America's] spiritual confusion, the Church's pastors should be able to detect an authentic thirst for God and for an intimate personal relationship with him.... Pastors must honestly ask whether they have paid sufficient attention to the thirst of the human heart for the true 'living water' which only Christ our redeemer can give."[5]

Christian insight meditation directly addresses "the spiritual renewal of the Church in the United States" (no. 5) called for by the Pope in his talk with the Midwestern bishops. It offers a sound Eastern meditation practice in the context of a reliable Christian prayer tradition. It helps Christians practice daily the moral and spiritual consequences of their religious faith. It disposes them for the ineffable gift of God's purifying and transforming love in contemplation.

Moreover, Christian insight meditation highlights the providential role of St. John of the Cross as a spiritual guide during this critical stage of the Church's growth and development in the United States. He teaches an authentic Vatican II spirituality. He is thoroughly Christocentric, leading us unhesitatingly into the mystery of Jesus' death and resurrection. At the same time he is completely Trinitarian.

John explains how the Holy Spirit, the living Flame of Love, transforms our lives into God's. He also details the practical implications for us of both the immanence and transcendence of the Incomprehensible Godhead. He thus serves as a bridge for dialogue with Eastern religions. He is a critical guide for assimilating from these religions practices that can enhance the growth of Christian contemplative life.

K.C.

Chapter 24

ON CONTEMPLATIVE PRAYER AND DOING INSIGHT PRACTICE

What is the relationship of Christian Insight Meditation to the Jesus Prayer? to Centering Prayer? to Christian Meditation (John Main)? to other forms of Christian contemplative prayer?

Chapter 21 explained that many types of Christian contemplative prayer exist. Yet, you may still wonder how watching the breath, body experiences, and mind-states (emotions, moods, states of awareness) can truly be called prayerful. Such honest concern needs an answer, but providing one requires some reflection. This chapter explains the difference between Christian insight meditation and these other contemplative practices.

Types of Prayer

First we must distinguish several types of prayer. A major distinction is between "talking prayer" and "listening prayer." When young, we were taught to "say our prayers," to pray by talking. We praised God, thanked God, apologized to God, and petitioned God for our own and others' needs. Sometimes this prayer was in formal, set words, and sometimes we improvised it, just talking to God about our lives and feelings.

All the forms of classical, non-discursive meditation are prayers of listening, of just making ourselves available to receive. They are usually quite simple, because we do not want to complicate listening prayer. Throughout this chapter we speak of meditation in this classical, Eastern understanding of it as a non-discursive practice; this usage corresponds closely to Western understandings of contemplative prayer.

Meditation is not just making the mind blank, though. Most of us lack the mental ability only to listen unless we have a "tool" to help us. Different types of meditation use different tools to keep attention sharp and clear while we listen. Simplicity is a grace of advanced practice; we cannot "force" it by trying to make the mind empty.

Some talking forms of prayer can be meditative; the words become mental anchoring devices that allow us to listen. This is true of much liturgy and some private devotions like the rosary and the stations of the cross, which involve repeating similar words. *Lectio divina* and *metta* practice ought be done meditatively. However, when these methods stir up thinking, which is mental speech, we are not practicing listening prayer. Such "thinking" work is usually called discursive meditation; John of the Cross so understood it.[1]

Many people discount the value of listening prayer, non-discursive meditation. It may feel like "doing nothing." So, for many Christians, prayer is only reciting formal words either in liturgical celebrations or in the rote repetition of memorized prayers. Those with greater intimacy in prayer may "tell God the news" or ask God for assistance.

Real conversation implies two-way interaction. It is not conversation when one person "hogs the floor." So, for prayer as St. Teresa of Avila defined it, as conversation with God, we must listen. When faced with one who has more to offer than we do, the greatest profit comes from mostly listening instead of getting in our own words. How much more true this should be of prayer! Mystics have frequently said that listening is much higher prayer. How much better off we are when we become still to hear God!

Types of Meditation

Classical meditation requires refraining from thinking to focus simple and complete awareness on some meditation object. We usually call such practice contemplative prayer. We close down the noise of words in surrendered openness and stop trying to control things by analyzing or problem solving. Such meditation falls into two basic types.

Concentrative meditation focuses attention upon a single object and excludes everything else; an image, icon, word, sound, the breath, a candle flame — almost any single object will do. As soon as we become aware of straying to anything else, we gently bring attention back to the object. Most Christian contemplative prayer is concentrative meditation.

In the second kind of meditation, uncovering or awareness meditation, we try to be aware with fresh observing of *all* we experience. Attention is constantly drawn to different objects to be noticed: emotions, body sensations, noises, and so on. In such practice, which this book has taught you, we can also stray from the task of clear awareness.

Many different useful techniques exist to do both forms of meditation. Both can eventually bring loving knowledge of God; they are simply different paths to this goal. My experience, however, shows insight meditation to be a particularly potent and direct method of purification for the nakedness of spirit needed for very deep experience of God. Teachers in other traditions have agreed with me.

Concentrative Meditation

Let us look at concentrative meditation in more detail. We hold attention on *one* particular object — a word, a sensory experience, an icon, an image. The object differs across traditions, and sometimes at different stages of practice. We close out everything else, more and more deeply experiencing that one object. In much Christian contemplative prayer, the object is often some form of Jesus' name that represents the presence of Jesus. A common Eastern object is a deity's "seed" syllable, similarly seen. Concentrative practice aims to transform the meditator into the object of focus.

Levels of concentration. Before concentration gets well established, the mind stays focused on its object for fleeting minutes before wandering off. With practice, these times become more and more pronounced; concentration deepens as we keep the mind centered on one object. Concentration has four major levels.[2]

When we can stay with the object for some time, the first level of concentration is achieved. The mind is held by the object, but might "circle around" it in simple thought. Ordinarily, discursive thought does not occur, although a clear image and some conceptual understanding of the object may be present.

The second level of concentration has no thought at all. A meditative word or words can be repeated, but thought about them ceases; we dwell "within" the object, which becomes a subtle point in the mind. This very delightful level of concentration is characterized by strong joy, "sweetness," and high energy. There may be pauses in the breath or peculiar patterns of breathing. Intense rapture and ecstatic awareness can occur.

A quite simple object of focus is needed for the third level of absorption. Joy falls off, leaving behind a pervasive, subtle happiness. Meditators are aware that attention is totally captivated by the object, seen more as a subtle essence than as a gross object. Sometimes we become unable to repeat the word or words upon which we are concentrating. Awareness of time and space may be lost or become distorted in perfectly attending to the object. Attention is so captivated that it may become impossible to move it to even a very exciting thought.

At the fourth level of concentration, awareness of time, space, and self may cease. All that exists in awareness is the object of concentration; the meditator has "disappeared" into the object. Even happiness fades, and all that remains is the one-pointed focus on the object with great stillness and balance of mind. Nothing is able to disturb the underlying calm of mind. The breath may cease for periods of time.

Christian prayer and concentration. The first level of concentrative absorption is like the Christian Prayer of Recollection. The intellect is captivated and no longer can do ordinary imaging and thinking. Christian contemplative prayer is said to begin when this occurs. We can reach the first level of absorption doing *lectio divina,* but only if we are more savoring rather than thinking about the scripture.

The second level of concentration parallels the Prayer of Quiet. Both share the same intense captivation and sweet joy. While some surface distractions may come, the object still holds us "underneath" them. Meditative experience strongly draws us, and we would like to spend long hours in it. A mantric prayer like the rosary can reach this level. It is often reached with *metta* and *mantra* practices like the Jesus Prayer, once the mind is sufficiently trained.

The third level parallels the Christian Prayer of Union. Both have great tranquility and stillness. Distraction is virtually impossible. Some forms of Christian prayer are too "busy" for this level; *metta* practice and the rosary can reach it. Simple *mantras* like the Jesus Prayer most easily carry us this far; they become a mere "ripple" in the mind. When we can no longer say the words, it may feel like concentration is lessening. However, this occurs because the mind has gone beyond any capacity for words.

The fourth level is like the Prayer of Espousal. Although it may be an anguished time in Christian practice and may mirror the intensity of advanced insight in Buddhist practice, still an unshakable poise and equanimity characterize it. The meditator is totally captivated by the experience. *Metta* practice and the rosary are too "gross" for this level; *mantras* become very subtle and more a point of consciousness than a fully formed word.

Uncovering or Insight Meditation

Unlike concentrative meditation, in uncovering meditation we accept into awareness as much of what happens as possible. The movement is almost exactly the opposite from concentrative meditation; practice will have many different objects. We do not choose our experiences; we let them choose us. We become willing to "hear" whatever is being said to us, to be with whatever experience comes. This is not just letting the mind wander, though; very disciplined methods guide the practice. You learned one of them in this book.

Common features of insight practice.   Along with awareness, this practice also develops concentration. Experiences differ from those of concentrative meditation, but follow the same general progression. The stages of insight practice were outlined in the discussion of Right Understanding in chapter 19.

Insight practice teaches us listening, how to become very still. It guides us in letting go of the noisy busyness of mind-chatter, of craving particular experiences in prayer, of wanting to be in charge of the conversation with God. It teaches us simply to be there, listening, surrendered to the purifying action of the Holy Spirit. It empties us of all that St. John of the Cross said must be emptied out to receive God's self-communication. We become docile and pliable before the Spirit.

What we "hear" in insight practice.   God usually first communicates self-knowledge, which John of the Cross said is the necessary road to God. We cannot know God if we do not know self. Since we already know what we are comfortable knowing about ourselves, most of the needed self-knowledge is painful. If we faithfully listen to this, God shows us even more; we get into the subtle recesses of deeply ingrained resistance to God's purifying action.

God then goes on to fill us with the gifts of the Holy Spirit, revealing things earthly and heavenly, even God's intimate secrets. As we more and more empty out, we can be more and more filled with God. Insight practice disposes us to stay empty before God's action.

As we let God work on and in us, God more and more purifies the unwholesome inclinations of mind and heart that keep us from God. The more we are willing, the more will God respond and effect the union of wills that transforms us. John of the Cross says that very few are willing to be radically surrendered before God, and to stay surrendered when the going gets hard. Insight meditation is a method for staying surrendered.

What is our goal? To become pure receptivity in the conversation with God, to hold nothing in the heart that is contrary to God's presence. As we empty out, God "inflows," and God's inflowing empties us out. John of the Cross speaks of this as a transformation that brings a union of likeness with God. When there is only God with all else emptied out, our knowing, our loving, and our experience is that of God. In its substance, the soul clings only to God.

Difficulties in Contemplative Practice

Early practice. Wandering mind happens frequently in early practice, both concentrative and awareness forms. Developing concentration is *not* easy, so we must not become discouraged. We simply bring the mind back to the practice "tool" — such as a sacred word or mental noting, the soft mental whisper naming our experience — whenever it wanders.

In concentrative practice, people often become bored with the sameness of experience. A difficulty in awareness practice is the discomfort of seeing much that had been hidden from awareness. Processes of both body and mind can be experienced very painfully. Patience and surrendered willingness are antidotes for both problems.

Middle practice. Once practice is fairly well developed, other problems are more likely. "Sinking mind" happens if we abandon the tool of practice — sacred word or noting — too soon. Once we feel really grounded, letting go of the tool is tempting. The mind can then go into a rather fuzzy, comfortable, amorphous state, but lacks the sharp, clear awareness needed for meditation. Because this state feels so good, we enjoy sinking into it; however, it is not meditation, and greed for it is a potent barrier to meditation.

St. Teresa was well aware of this problem and warned against it.[3] The cure is to repeat the sacred word or noting until the mind is so captivated by the object that it becomes absolutely impossible to use this tool. John Main, who studied with an Indian yogi, clearly understood how important this is, and his instructions reflect that knowledge.

A second problem in concentrative practice is also caused by letting the mind get empty before it is entirely captivated. If you let go of the meditative object, unconscious mental contents might rush up. This experience can be very frightening and overwhelming, so you should hold fast to the object used as a tool. Concentrative practice ordinarily brings unconscious upsurges only when the mind is so completely balanced that it can handle them. It is not designed to deal with this state prematurely.

Awareness practice *is* meant to deal with our unfinished business, so such things occur earlier in it. We must be careful, though, to keep up the noting. This protects us from getting lost in any content, but still allows us to experience it fully for healing. Awareness meditators are sometimes tempted to get lost in analyzing these experiences; they become fascinated by inner mental contents and want to wallow in them. Yielding to this temptation derails practice.

Summary

Most methods of Christian contemplative prayer, such as the many forms of the Jesus Prayer, are technically called concentrative meditation techniques. Such practice gradually transforms the meditator into the object of focus. We must remember to hold on to this meditation tool until it becomes impossible to do so.

Insight meditation is awareness practice, which draws up the impurities in the mind and heart to be healed by the Wisdom that guides the practice. It is often less pleasant, but seems to move people more quickly toward their goal. Since John of the Cross encouraged this aim in his work, we recommend awareness practice as a method for his spirituality.

Both concentrative and awareness methods are prayers of deep listening to God. Both dispose us for contemplation.

M.J.M.

Chapter 25

ON OTHER FORMS
OF CHRISTIAN PRAYER

How does Christian insight meditation relate to other forms of Christian Prayer like liturgy, *lectio divina,* private devotions, and the practice of presence of God? Does it complement them? Does it replace them?

Pray Always

Christian insight meditation, like any other contemplative practice, intends to strengthen our entire prayer life and help us to live always in communion with God. Jesus taught us "to pray continually" (Lk 18:1). Over the centuries Christians have responded to his challenge in various ways that express the total human person as a body/spirit, social/private being. The Church throughout the world is now always at prayer, although we are not always praying in the same way. The goal of all Christian prayer, however, remains the same: continual communion with God and transformation of our lives in Christ.

Liturgy.   Liturgy is our primary communal prayer, especially Eucharist and the sacraments. There we pray socially, as a community of faith. We gather together in the Risen Lord to remember what he did for us in his life, death, and resurrection. We open ourselves to receive the fruits of his life-giving death. We become incorporated into the Lord's risen body. We are nourished and sustained by his word and his body and blood. We experience Christ's healing touch restoring us to wholeness. We receive his strength to meet life's challenges and fulfill our social commitments as his disciples.

We experience ourselves being gradually transformed in Christ as, year after year, we participate in the Church's liturgical cycles celebrating his life, death, resurrection, ascension, and the sending of his Spirit. As we repeatedly recall the great events that gave us new life in Christ, we ask the Father to "bring the image of your Son to perfection within us" (Preface of Lent, I).

Lectio Divina. Closely associated with liturgy is *lectio divina*. This prayerful reading of Sacred Scripture is itself an ancient and powerful form of contemplative prayer. The meditative reading of the Old and New Testaments allows God's word to sink deeply into our hearts, transforming us into Christ, the Scripture's fulfillment.

Devotions. Christian prayer has many popular devotions and private prayers that express our human needs to God. One of the most popular, the way of the cross, allows us to identify the struggles of our own life with the Lord's suffering and death. The rosary recalls Mary of Nazareth, Jesus' mother and ours, who models faithful Christian discipleship and openness to the Holy Spirit. Beyond these, literally countless public and private prayers and devotions help us to adore, praise, thank, and petition God.

Presence of God. One particularly important Christian prayer is the "practice of the presence of God," a phrase associated with Brother Lawrence of the Resurrection, a seventeenth-century French Carmelite lay brother. In this prayer, we attempt simply to be aware of God's presence in every moment of our day, in every activity and occupation. We look for God nowhere else than in this present moment, regardless of what we are doing.

Brother Lawrence said he found God, not only in formal prayer in church, but especially among the pots and pans in the monastery kitchen where for years he prepared his brothers' meals. Lawrence considered it "a big mistake to think that the period of mental prayer should be different from any other. We must be just as closely united with God during our activities as we are during our times of prayer."[1]

Summary. This brief survey hardly does justice to the varieties of Christian prayer throughout two millennia; however, it illustrates the Church's response to Jesus' instruction to pray always and its desire for continual communion with God. The different forms of contemplative prayer mentioned in chapter 21 do not diminish this rich variety, but continually bring new life and depth to it. Insight meditation does so in several ways.

Christian Insight Meditation

Purifying our hearts and reforming our lives each day according to the Gospel make our prayer pleasing to God. "It is not those who say to me, 'Lord, Lord,' who will enter the kingdom of heaven, but the person who does the will of my Father in heaven" (Mt 7:21). We try during daily mental prayer to empty sense and spirit completely and surrender ourselves totally into God's hands as Jesus did on Calvary. This prepares us fully for liturgy, where we celebrate Jesus' paschal mystery and apply its fruits to our lives.

Regular attention to the breath develops a growing consciousness of the presence of the Spirit whom Jesus breathes upon us. It readies us to follow where the Spirit leads, even into unfamiliar territory. "The wind blows wherever it pleases; you hear its sound, but you cannot tell where it comes from or where it is going. That is how it is with all who are born of the Spirit" (Jn 3:8).

The meditation discipline of staying in the present moment, refusing to give mental energy to thoughts of the past or the future, trains us for moment-to-moment attention to the here and now. This enables us to live fully in God's presence as we involve ourselves in the endless tasks that make up our day. "Do not worry about tomorrow," Jesus reminds us, "for tomorrow will have its own worries. Let each day's problems be sufficient for the day" (Mt 6:34).

Daily Meditation

Insight meditation enlivens our prayer life only to the extent that we meditate every day. The Buddhist and Carmelite traditions agree solidly on this: to experience fully the fruits of meditation you must meditate every day. Where? How long? That depends on you.

Obviously, you cannot follow the daily meditation schedule of an intensive retreat in your everyday life. You must, however, make a commitment to meditate every day. The more time you can practice, the better. Two hours a day is better than one hour, one hour better than twenty minutes. Realistically, most find that from a half-hour to an hour daily is possible, even in the most demanding of daily schedules.

Some find that a half-hour in the morning and another half-hour in the evening works best for them. Others can meditate only once a day, usually in the morning, but do so for forty-five minutes to an hour. You should begin by setting aside at least a half-hour a day for meditation. Once you determine when and how long, stick to it. Every day. That's the secret. Gradually meditation becomes as routine a part of your day as going to bed at night and getting up in the morning. Soon you will begin to experience its benefits — less tension, more peace, better prayer, and gradually the transformation of your life.

Is there any time of day better than any other for meditation? The best time is when you can do it regularly so that it consistently becomes a normal part of your day. Some people find right after meals or late in the day more difficult.

But experiment to learn which are the better or poorer times for you.

To enliven one's entire prayer life, I recommend meditation immediately before reading Sacred Scripture or celebrating Eucharist. This prepares the heart to hear God's word in new ways and sets the stage for new insight into the deeper meanings of the words and symbols you celebrate in worship.

Herbert Benson's research suggests that sitting quietly, comfortably, passively or without discursive reflection, and paying attention to your breathing just before religious exercises frees your brain to form new neural connections that physiologically mediate new meaning and insight.[2] Meditation literally prepares you physiologically to get the most benefit from spiritual reading and liturgical worship.

Christian insight meditation thus aims to enrich rather than replace other forms of Christian prayer. Often, to make time for meditation, persons discontinue some other prayers or devotional practices. But they also discover a deepening in their remaining prayer, especially liturgy, sacred reading, and the practice of the presence of God. They find "a pearl of great price" (Mt 13:45–46) that gives new life to their desire to pray always.

                                                              K.C.

Chapter 26

ON CARMELITE PRAYER

Do Carmelite saints like John of the Cross and Teresa of Jesus specifically teach this method of meditation? What is the relationship of insight meditation to the Carmelite tradition of prayer?

Although Carmelite authors agree on many essential elements of contemplative prayer, they do not give us one specific Carmelite method of meditation. They are very free in their approach to meditation and respect the many ways in which the Holy Spirit leads us in prayer.

Carmelite teachers of prayer, especially Teresa of Jesus and John of the Cross, do not explicitly describe insight meditation as taught in this book. However, their teachings on contemplative prayer reveal some remarkable similarities with insight meditation. When approached with an attitude of faith in God's indwelling presence and an ardent desire to be lovingly present to God, insight meditation provides a practice that integrates much of what Teresa and John teach about the heart of true prayer. We see this when we explore their essential teachings on prayer.

St. Teresa

St. Teresa defines prayer as "intimate sharing between friends; it means taking time frequently to be alone with Him who we know loves us."[1] With utter simplicity, she explains her early method of entering into this loving relationship with God: "I tried as hard as I could to keep Jesus

Christ, our God and our Lord, present within me, and this was my way of prayer."[2]

Wrong understanding. A first reading of Teresa's way of prayer might make us think that when she prayed she kept within her a mental image of Jesus, such as Jesus dying on the cross, and that this mental picture was the object of her meditation. We might also think that she spent her prayer time pondering the teachings of Jesus or the spiritual life, and from her reflections drew out beautiful thoughts and resolutions to apply to her life. This is an incorrect understanding of Teresa's manner of prayer.

In the same passage where Teresa explains her method of prayer, she confesses that, no matter how hard she tied, she never had the talent for discursive reflection nor the type of imagination that could picture the humanity of Jesus Christ. A few chapters later in her autobiography, she says that she was unable to represent things with the intellect. She could only think of Christ as he was as man, but she could not picture him within herself despite all she read about his beauty and the many images she saw of him. She compares herself to a blind person or someone in the dark. They speak with a person and know that the person is with them because they believe that the other is there, although they do not see the other.[3]

Teresa's way. When she writes that she tried as hard as she could to keep Jesus Christ present within her, she means that she strove to become conscious of the Spirit of the Risen Christ within her heart and to remain there in his presence. She entered prayer with an attitude of deep faith in the presence of Christ and the simple ardent desire to love him and "to be his companion."[4]

To remain interiorly centered on the presence of Christ, Teresa needed an anchor for her wandering mind. Although she mentions several ways of recollecting herself, such as using a picture of Christ or looking at nature, most often

Scripture provided a useful tool for concentration. She might read a passage from the Gospels like Jesus in the Garden of Olives, and place herself in the scene next to Jesus, remaining there at his side trying to console him by her loving presence.[5]

If she read the passage of the Samaritan woman at the well, she herself would become the Samaritan woman longing for the living water Jesus promised. Far from trying to develop elaborate reflections from the Gospel scenes, Teresa read the Scripture texts as a way to focus attention within to the presence of Christ. Once she made contact with Christ, she simply remained quietly and lovingly in his presence. However, as Teresa's mystical life deepened she became conscious of God's presence without any effort on her part. God's presence was more and more revealed to her and she became more passively quiet.

Teresa's "method." Teresa's inability to meditate discursively caused her much suffering for many years. When she prayed, her distracted mind ran like a millclapper. Out of this experience and to help people with the same difficulty, she taught the prayer of recollection in chapter 26 of *The Way of Perfection*. This is Teresa's "method" of meditation. She states that the Lord taught her this method and one makes greater progress following it than meditating with the intellect.[6]

Fundamental to this way of prayer is the faith conviction that God dwells in the depths of our hearts. It is there that we seek God. "Consider what St. Augustine says, that he sought him in many places but found him ultimately within himself. Do you think it matters little for a soul with a wandering mind to understand this truth and see that there is no need to go to heaven in order to speak with one's Eternal Father or find delight in Him? ... All one need do is go into solitude and look at Him within oneself."[7]

Once God's presence is remembered, the next movement is interior. We collect our senses and faculties together and direct our attention within to be with God.[8] This movement is one of faith and love directed toward a personal encounter with God.

When we enter within ourselves to be with God, what do we do? Teresa directs us to "look at" Christ. She is not asking us to think about him or to draw out concepts or make subtle reflections with the intellect. All she asks is that we "look at him." For Teresa, to look at Christ is an act of faith and love. It is loving attention to the presence of Christ within. It may or may not involve words. What is most essential is to be with Christ.

The heart of Teresian prayer. This loving attention to Christ touches the heart of Teresian prayer. In *The Book of Her Foundations,* Teresa teaches that our progress in prayer lies not in thinking much, but in loving much.[9] She repeats the same thought in *The Interior Castle.* "The important thing is not to think much but to love much; and so do that which best stirs you to love."[10]

St. Teresa is quite clear, however, that attention to God within may not necessarily be consoling or pleasurable. The silent, loving "look" at Christ may take place in dryness and aridity. We may experience God's presence as absence; we may find it difficult to quiet our restless mind. Essential is the attitude of faith and love we bring to prayer.

Entering within herself in order to be lovingly attentive to the divine guest dwelling within expresses most precisely and simply Teresa's method of prayer. Love is the essence of prayer, not thinking. An attitude of faith must also permeate prayer because we may not experience spiritual consolations when we meditate.

St. John of the Cross

Because he was primarily interested in teaching the nature of contemplation, John of the Cross does not give us detailed instructions on how to meditate. Rather, he tells us how to empty ourselves to grow in relationship with God and describes the purifying effects of contemplation.

John says very little about discursive meditation. He refers to it only in those texts where he describes the prayer of beginners or discusses the movement from meditation as discursive reflection with the intellect and senses toward a more passive form of contemplative prayer.[11] John understood discursive meditation as a passing, transitory phase. Its main purpose is to gain a deeper knowledge and love of Jesus Christ. It helps beginners on the spiritual path to become more interior. It brings them to a sensible awareness and knowledge of God's love for them that leads to further conversion and detachment.[12]

Emptying for contemplation. John does not teach us the mechanics of meditation, but he offers much on how to empty ourselves in order to be filled with God. His major concern in his writings is to help us dispose ourselves for the gift of contemplation.

He teaches us to disencumber ourselves in prayer and life from activities that impede a loving awareness of God's presence and the purifying action of the Holy Spirit. He believed that God is ever present like the sun above us always ready to communicate its beneficent rays.[13] To receive those rays, we must unclutter and clear the ground of our heart of all that obstructs the action of God's Spirit within us. John assures us that if we do our part to surrender to God's transforming presence we will experience the liberating love of the Spirit through contemplation.

To surrender to God's gracious presence in contemplative prayer, John believed that we must undergo a conversion in how we naturally commune with God. God is a mystery of love. God is both intimately close to us, yet beyond all we can think, feel, or conceive. God communicates with us in a supernatural way that transcends our natural faculties of thinking, loving, feeling, and acting. That is why we can never judge God's presence or absence in our lives by our feelings or the beautiful thoughts we may have about God. God communicates with us secretly through "a simple, loving knowledge" that is peaceful, quiet, and serene (F3, 34).

Bases for contemplation.   Contemplation, which John defines as loving knowledge of God infused within us secretly, quietly, and obscurely, is God's pure gift. We can neither earn it nor attain it through our natural faculties of knowing, loving, or acting. We receive it passively.

We dispose ourselves to receive this gift by communing with God according to God's mode of communing with us — quietly, serenely, and peacefully. We lay aside our natural active mode and become receivers, not givers; passive, not active. In prayer, we let go of our desire to do something, to feel God's presence, to make subtle reflections about God, and to control our relationship with God. Instead, John instructs us to become idle, passive, and tranquil in God's presence.[14]

Loving attention.   When John discusses the movement from discursive meditation to contemplation in *The Ascent of Mount Carmel* and *The Living Flame of Love*, he encourages a prayer of loving attention. "Spiritual persons... should learn to remain in God's presence with loving attention and a tranquil intellect, even though they seem to themselves to be idle" (A2, 15, 5). We must conduct ourselves passively in God's presence, without efforts of our own other than a simple loving awareness, "as when opening one's eyes with loving attention" (F3, 33).

Disposing the soul.   To remain in God's presence with loving awareness gradually brings about a divine calm and peace that disposes us for a sublime loving knowledge of God that God infuses within us. John maintains that pacifying the soul, making it calm and peaceful, inactive and desireless, is no small accomplishment, for it is an essential disposition for contemplation.

Nevertheless, we naturally want to be active in our relationship with God and to keep our minds busy chattering and grasping for ideas. Becoming idle and tranquil in God's presence is difficult. The prayer of loving attention implies self-emptying.[15]

It invites us to surrender our craving for self-gratifying experiences, to lay aside our compulsive thinking, and simply to remain in God's presence in peace and quiet, with simple loving awareness. But when we do so, God will not fail to communicate with us, silently and secretly. It is more impossible than it would be "for the sun not to shine on clear and uncluttered ground" (F3, 46). This is what our Lord asks of us through the prophet David: "Learn to be empty of all things — interiorly and exteriorly — and you will behold that I am God" (A2, 15, 5).

Insight Meditation

Our examination of Teresa and John's ways of prayer reveals several similarities between the Carmelite tradition of prayer and insight meditation. When approached with faith in God's indwelling presence and a desire to be lovingly present to God, insight practice can help us integrate some of their essential and fundamental teachings on contemplative prayer.

Loving presence to God. First of all, in both Teresa and John, the essence of contemplative prayer is loving presence to God, not thinking. Although Teresa encouraged the use of Scripture or a picture of Christ as an aid to concentration and for bringing us to an awareness of Christ's presence, her way of prayer is essentially a loving presence to Christ who dwells within us.

We find the same teaching in John's discussion of the prayer of loving attention. He stresses the importance of learning to remain in God's presence with simple, loving awareness. This pacifies the soul, which, John emphasizes, is no small accomplishment, for it allows God, the principle agent in prayer, to infuse divine loving knowledge into our lives.[16]

Awareness and the present moment. Insight meditation develops an ever-deepening awareness. As a contemplative practice, it teaches us to recollect ourselves and direct
attention to the present moment where alone we find God.
Remaining in the present moment with clear and simple
awareness quiets and calms the mind and heart, creating a
listening, empty, and receptive space for God's creative action
in our lives.

Self-emptying.   Another similarity between Carmelite
prayer and insight practice concerns the self-emptying process. We refer primarily to John of the Cross's teaching that
we must become empty in order to be filled with God. "God
does not fit in an occupied heart" (F3, 48).

We must do our part to free our hearts and minds from
inadequate and distorted ideas and concepts about the Incomprehensible God, from desires for self-gratification in
prayer, and from activities that prevent the peaceful inflow of
God's loving presence into our hearts. We must learn to become passive, idle, tranquil, and lovingly attentive to God's
presence. This requires letting go of our natural activity of
knowing, loving, and feeling to allow God's purifying love to
awaken and transform us.

Insight meditation as a path of purification is a powerful means to bring about the emptiness about which John
writes. It directs us to silence our chattering minds, to surrender our craving for sensible satisfaction, and to rest from
our compulsive need to do something in prayer.

Insight practice teaches us to become passive, idle, tranquil, and empty in God's presence. By surrendering to this
moment's experience with bare and simple attention and letting go of obsessive thinking and ideas — holy as they may
be — and of emotional states — delightful as they may feel —
we become empty, receptive, and disposed for the gift of
contemplation.

                                                        D.C.

Chapter 27

ON PSYCHOLOGICAL FACTORS IN MEDITATION

Isn't this form of meditation psychologically dangerous? How does this practice compare with contemporary systems of Western psychology and psychotherapy? Isn't this just a mind game, manipulating your mind?

Problems That Are Not Problems

The fears expressed in these questions are understandable. Sometimes meditators are concerned about things that are not real problems, however. Much of this worry has no factual basis, once we understand more fully what is happening.

Self-manipulation. We are not isolated "parts" — spirit, mind, emotions, body — in how we function; we work as an integrated unit. What affects any part of our being affects all of our being. Whether we choose to do it consciously or not, we often effect changes in different parts of our being for various purposes.

Using psychological methods to assist the aims of prayer has a time-honored place in spiritual traditions. Some methods have even produced real trauma but have been counted worth it when they fostered spiritual goals. Medieval mystics frequently used severe fasts, self-flagellation, vigils, and so on, to bring psychological effects. Psychological changes are not sought for their own sake, but to make us "ripe" to receive grace.

Using a psychologically sound method, which has proven
itself over twenty-five-hundred years, should not cause
alarm. We know that it is simply a tool to help us be surrendered and listening. We cannot force God, but we *can* do
all possible to prepare the ground for God's communication
of grace.

Hallucinations. Meditators sometimes hallucinate — see
when there is no visual stimulus, hear without an auditory
stimulus. Some fear they are losing their minds, but many
situations make such things happen. We hallucinate every
night when we dream. People see mirages in the desert and
have sensory experiences in intense isolation. Some illnesses
create sensory experience. St. Teresa of Avila complained of
a cacophony of noise in her head, and probably suffered
from tinnitus. Meditation is just one of many causes of such
events. Some people hallucinate even early in meditation
practice.

Hallucinations do occur in some mental illness. Mentally disordered persons usually believe the sensory event has
physical reality, while meditators tend to realize otherwise.
Although hallucinations should not alarm us, we also should
not seek them. St. John of the Cross repeatedly urged meditators to place no importance on such experiences, but to hold
to "purity of spirit in dark faith — the means toward union"
(A2, 19, 14).

Auditory experiences in meditation often begin with a
sound like surf. We can also hear very loud bells and chimes,
and even human voices. Visual experiences can be of lights,
colors, geometrical symbols, faces, scenes, and so on. Meditators may sometimes feel like something is touching or
pulling them, and some smell peculiar odors and taste un-
usual tastes.

The body also can feel greatly distorted. Body parts may
feel like they are in the wrong place in the body. Some parts
may feel ballooned out or grotesquely large, while others feel

flattened out or squashed. Deepening concentration causes such distortions.

Rapture. A wide range of body sensations called rapture sometimes happen. They come from having strong concentration and interested focus on the object of meditation practice. Some rapture is extremely pleasurable and other intensely painful. Sometimes a startling mixture of pleasure and pain occurs. St. Teresa said, "Since the pain is sweet and delightful, we never think we can have enough of this pain."[1] In her well-known transverberation experience, when an angel pierced her with a spear, she reported a paradoxical mix of pain and great sweetness. She wrote at length about rapture, and St. John of the Cross also discussed it.

St. John also wrote about sensual movements that sometimes occur spontaneously during spiritual practice; he clearly seems to be speaking of sexual arousal. When rapture is very intense, prolonged waves of orgasmic sensation may flood the body with intense bliss. Skin can become so sensitive that even a faint breeze across the cheek can trigger waves of orgasm. Hindu yogis, who have studied such phenomena for millennia, explain that although all our vital energy is connected, these experiences are spiritual rather than sexual ones.

Rapture also comes as intense heaviness, or as being pushed or pulled strongly in one direction. Involuntary movements can occur. St. Teresa also knew about these; she wrote: "Some persons say they experience a tightening in the chest and even external bodily movements that they cannot restrain."[2] The force of such movements can even bounce a person off the meditation seat. Various powers and energies may activate, like the *kundalini* experience of yoga. It can feel like an exorcism is being performed on the meditator.

Meditators prone to intense rapture should be guided by a competent teacher who understands such experiences so they can learn how to work with these events. They should not cling to them or encourage them, but also not try to push them away, all the while staying balanced and equanimous.

If rapture is improperly managed, we may overvalue it. We can easily become greedy for striking experiences, often very subtly so, and impede further spiritual progress. St. John of the Cross said the weakness of human nature causes rapture: "The sensory part of the soul is weak and incapable of vigorous spiritual communications [so] these proficients, because of such communications experienced in the sensitive part, suffer many infirmities, injuries, and weaknesses of stomach, and as a result fatigue of spirit" (N2, 1, 2).

Meditation and Healing the Psyche

Bodily conditions. Meditation practice allows the body to release traumas it has been harboring. Once during practice, intense pain suddenly radiated up from my tail bone. After watching it a while, a strong memory of being kicked very hard in the tail bone came abruptly. With the memory, the pain stopped. Before then, I had periods of tenderness in the area about twice a year, and never knew why. I have not had any tail bone pain since that time. The body seems to hold some memory of traumas that have not been sufficiently attended; allowing them into awareness in practice lets the body fully experience and release them.

Thinking. Thinking is a mixed activity. Although it can create a lot of suffering for ourselves and others, it also is a very useful tool for dealing with matter. If we want to build a bridge that will stay up, creating models of it in thought helps; we can test their workability before actually putting up the bridge. But in spiritual practice or dealing with relationships, thought is more often a problem than a help.

When we create concepts, we solidify experiences, making them solid and permanent in mind. Once we decide that we suffer from something called depression, then it is always lurking, always waiting to claim us. We no longer simply have times when energy is down and we feel sad. Depression continues to "exist" even when we are feeling quite satisfied and can always threaten to erupt. We suffer from it even when not suffering it.

We do this to people, too. We develop an impression of them, and then insist that they are like our image. They may have changed greatly, but our preconceived picture — you can call it a prejudice — keeps us from seeing them as they now are. We respond to them through this prejudging, and they most often respond back according to how we treated them. When we can see them more clearly, we may have much more satisfying dealings.

Practice makes us very aware of the difference between really experiencing something and thinking about it or living in concepts about it. As we become skilled in seeing how we make concepts, which is one fruit of meditation practice, we can stop doing so when it is not helpful. We thus become free of much mind-created misery. Meditation also helps us stay more focused on tasks, so we save a lot of time formerly wasted in distractions.

Emotion. Almost all of us have unfinished emotional business. Experiences that we were too immature, too vain, or too vulnerable to handle when they occurred do not go away simply because we did not deal with them. They seem locked into our beings — not only mentally, but also in body tissue. The healing process is seen very clearly in psychosomatic disturbances, bodily problems with a recognized psychological cause.

Meditation practice loosens the barriers that have kept down experiences of emotional pain. Often quite early in meditation practice, emotional material starts to surface. From whatever we diverted our attention, whatever we refused to see when it first occurred, whatever vanity or immaturity or fear made it impossible for us to see — all of this gets shaken loose. Some people complain that meditation is not good for them because it makes them feel angry, tense, anxious, or bored. Meditation cannot make us feel any of this; it only reveals what is already there, the proclivities of mind hidden from view.

Storms of very intense emotion can flood the meditator. Some feelings that emerge stay for a short time, others longer. The practice offers a method for dealing with all of it. We simply watch it move through without identifying with it. We do not consider it "mine," or get lost in it or carried away by it. Emotions are all impermanent like everything else, as this practice teaches, and eventually will cease.

These are not ordinary emotional storms, however. If we observe them according to the method taught, healing occurs. When the experience has been worked through, it truly works its way out. Eventually it goes, and it is gone — *really* gone, not to return again. The relief and lightness that follow release from the burden of emotional knots can be quite astonishing. Very often the change in us is readily apparent to others who know us fairly well.

Throughout early adulthood I felt that depression was just around the corner. During my first insight meditation retreat, I quickly hit an ocean of rage and sadness that lasted unabated for days. I could not report on practice to a teacher without bursting into tears, and I spent much other time crying. I wanted a god I could curse for all the misery in the world. The teachers kept me on track, carefully doing the practice. Finally these mind-states lifted, and I felt incredibly light. After the retreat friends and colleagues, even my children, rather tentatively said things like, "You're different. I can't quite put my finger on it, but different." Eventually, independently of each other, the consensus verdict was "softer, gentler, less pushed." They were correct.

The practice first releases personal unfinished emotional business. Then it also gets to the emotion-laden existential issues with which all humans must deal: aloneness, vulnerability, powerlessness, and personal emptiness. Typically we get to these "big four" in their greatest depth only after we have done considerable personal emotional clearing. Then work goes back and forth between personal and cosmic issues.

Emotional work is harrowing for some people. However, the practice is intelligent; if we use common sense, it does not give us more than we can handle at any time. If we work carefully, we can remain objective, as the practice requires. When the mind grows stronger and more spacious, more intense material can surface because we can stay balanced while experiencing it.

An occasional person reports feeling overcome with emotion while or after doing insight practice. The common cause for this is failing to do the practice as taught. Anyone feeling overwhelmed during or after practice should consult a teacher for help.

Psychotherapy and meditation.   People with severe psychiatric histories can successfully do insight meditation; many have. They should inform the teacher of their history before doing an intensive retreat to insure getting the guidance they may need.

Many psychiatric labels simply name different ways that people can become trapped in unhelpful self-understandings. Most people with disturbed emotion or thinking do not consciously know they hold these harmful opinions; the unaware understandings may even contradict their conscious experience. These distorted understandings also often control self-management and create tremendous suffering for everyone they affect.

For example, anorexics see themselves as too fat, even though they may be seriously underweight. Hypochondriacs carefully monitor body sensations and interpret slight changes as having medical importance. Depressed people usually automatically see things in negative ways, leaving themselves unable to find joy anywhere; commonly they are not even aware of the maladaptive patterns of thought that create their unhappiness. Many "normal" people create self-blaming attitudes, seeing self as inadequate or bad.

The *Dhammapada* opens by saying that mind is the forerunner of all things. As we see the workings of the mind and learn how to be healed of its unhelpful activities, we get firsthand experience of this truth. The mind creates the reality in which we live, and often we create realities that lead to great suffering and are quite removed from objective reality.

Meditation practice is like psychotherapy in healing many of these conditions. The purgative process is often difficult and painful, as good psychotherapy also can be. One young woman commented, after a three-week retreat, that she felt like she had been in intensive therapy for years.

Ultimately, meditation practice has a spiritual purpose and is not a psychotherapy. Whatever benefits of physical and mental health come, they are not the highest goal. Such mental "cleaning" is an integral part of the purgative process, though, since we function as a unit and not as separate parts. Healing any aspect of one's being brings healing of the total being. Our understanding of God remains very incomplete so long as we still cling to unwholesome psychological patterns.

Sometimes practice uncovers intense trauma of which we had been unaware. When this happens, combining meditation practice with psychotherapy produces the most rapid healing. When therapy is called for, we cannot expect the practice to do its work, just as we do not expect it to replace our physicians. The practice will fine-tune and polish gains made in therapy, and puts the finishing touches on psychotherapeutic work. The deep healing of meditation practice deals primarily with issues beyond the reach of therapy.

Summary

This form of practice is psychologically very sound. It is safe to do, since the tool of noting protects us from being swamped by intense experiences. It may produce some striking experiences, but these are not a problem just because they do not occur in ordinary daily living.

The practice heals the whole being. It clears away unfinished personal business so that we can be emptied of the trappings of self that bar the full inflowing of God. It makes us capable of receiving all that God would give us.

M.J.M.

Chapter 28

ON GETTING GUIDANCE IN PRACTICE

Is a spiritual guide necessary to practice this form of meditation? Where does one find guidance for this approach to prayer? Can I do this practice by myself if I don't live near a teacher?

Aids to Practicing Awareness Meditation

Awareness practice can easily be done without much teacher help except at critical periods. There are, however, some aids available that greatly support practice.

Initial learning. This meditation practice is most easily learned in a retreat taught by a competent teacher, since you can practice with guidance immediately available. The second easiest way is in a class, with instructions given over a six- to eight-week period. You can get a good start from written materials, however, as presented in this book.

If working only from written materials, be very careful not to try to do too much at once but to introduce the practice gradually. This allows you to consolidate learning at every step. If you decide to make awareness meditation part of your life, other aids like retreats help support practice.

Retreats. Insight meditators should sit a week-long retreat at least annually. If you do only weekend retreats, try to do two or more a year. Retreats deepen practice by offering an opportunity for continuous, mindful, concentrated awareness. Being free of other regular concerns allows the mind to penetrate more deeply into experience. Because attention is not dispersed, concentrated focus comes more rapidly.

Resources for Ecumenical Spirituality holds Silence and Awareness retreats regularly, teaching awareness practice as a method for the spirituality of John of the Cross. To get on their mailing list, write: RES, P.O. Box 6, Mankato, MN 56002–0006.

RES also has a forest monastery in Missouri, where people can arrange stays of varying lengths. Practice there can be more intensive than in daily life, but less rigorous than a retreat. A teacher is not available year around, so arrangements must be made in advance. Write: RES, Route 1, Box 1160, Dunnegan, MO 65640–9705.

Buddhist settings offer many awareness retreats. Sitting insight practice with Buddhist teachers can be a very good experience for Christians. Although such retreats do not include Christian experience, many fine teachers lead them. One special place is Insight Meditation Society, 1230 Pleasant Street, Barre MA 01005; they will put you on their mailing list on request.

Other retreats are available around the country. A good resource for locating retreats is *Inquiring Mind* newspaper, discussed below.

Sitting groups. To maintain practice day to day, a sitting group really helps. Sitting in meditation regularly with other people committed to the practice supports and nurtures the practice. *Inquiring Mind* also lists sitting groups around the country.

Sitting groups meet as frequently as their members want. They usually start with a thirty- to sixty-minute meditation sitting. After that, members sometimes simply disperse. Some visit with each other, some study together, and some have a teacher who offers material. What the group does should be decided by the wishes of its members.

You can start a sitting group if there is not one near you. Its members do not all have to do the same practice, so long as they sit in silent meditation together. The study could be of general spiritual teachings. Groups work best when they are flexible about attendance. Our local group meets twice weekly; some meditators come every meeting, some once a week, and some only occasionally.

Published materials. *Inquiring Mind* is a twice-yearly publication of the *vipassana* community that offers articles on various forms of awareness practice. It also lists retreats offered worldwide and sitting groups in different areas. They will send it to anyone who asks but request a donation toward covering costs from those who can afford it. Contact them at P.O. Box 9999, North Berkeley Station, Berkeley CA 94709.

The Washington Province of the Discalced Carmelite friars publishes *Spiritual Life,* a quarterly offering articles on Carmelite spirituality. Contact them at 2131 Lincoln Rd. N.E., Washington, DC 20002.

The 1991 Silence and Awareness retreat was published by Credence Cassettes (P.O. Box 419491, Kansas City MO 64141-6491; telephone: 1-800-333-7373). Listening to the instructions on tape and to lectures exploring the teaching of St. John in the light of awareness practice can help those not sitting with a teacher. Credence has also published additional work of Culligan and Meadow; these include more Silence and Awareness talks by Meadow.[1]

Tapes from other teachers in the Buddhist community are also available. Insight Meditation Society teachers offer tapes through Dharma Seed Tape Library, Box 66, Wendell Depot, MA 01380. Reading other books on practice is helpful, too. Some resources for reading materials were given in chapter 2 of this book (see above pp. 36–37).

Daily life. Most important for maintaining practice is the daily sitting. The ordinary sitting in awareness practice is forty-five to sixty minutes long. However, if you are not willing to invest that much time, decide how long you are willing to sit and make a commitment to sit daily for that long. You should sit whether you feel like it or not on any particular day, or you will miss valuable learning experiences.

People often ask about the best time of day to sit. This varies from person to person. Some people find attention less sharp soon after eating or late in the day. Others are not bothered by this. Most important is to have a regular time in your schedule for practice. When meditators try to "work it in" whenever they can, it very soon gets worked out. Many people make sitting part of their morning "getting up" routine. Other common times are before eating lunch or right after getting home from work before starting any other task.

As you start to see benefits in your life from the practice, you will become willing to sit for longer periods. You will realize that meditation makes time for itself. The time it saves us in emotional turmoil, unfocused mind, and sluggish energy more than makes up for the time it takes. Many people need less sleep when meditating regularly.

I recommend making a six-month commitment to do the practice regularly. By that time, you should see some benefits. It may not become your preferred spiritual practice, but unless you give it a chance to show what it can do, you will never know how much it might help.

Practice is greatly enhanced if you take odd minutes during the day to call yourself back to mindful awareness. You may use some act that you do frequently during the day, such as turning or reaching, as a signal to be mindful. You might choose to do some regular activity, such as washing dishes, walking to the office, or brushing teeth, with very careful mindfulness. Thich Nhat Hanh makes bell sounds a call to mindfulness.

Suggestions for Continuing Practice

All the aids suggested will help you maintain a practice. Let us now look at some other things to consider.

Method. Once learned, this practice is safe to do on your own if you meditate no more than several hours a day. To practice intensively for many hours a day, you should be under the guidance of a teacher; intensive practice can bring up very powerful experiences that might be emotionally unsettling.

The main thing the teacher will do, however, is remind you to use the method carefully, as you were taught it. So often we want to play around with methods, change them to suit personal inclinations. This method has proven itself over time. Using it faithfully and consistently brings the results it promises. Since it is not "broken," do not "fix" it. If you alter vital parts of it, you may waste time or get lost in upsetting experiences. The method both allows the purifying healing to occur and protects us while it is being done.

The second thing a teacher offers is reassurance. If you remember to use the method, you need not worry about what happens in your practice. Various experiences that you do not understand may come, and some of them may even be frightening. You will be fine if you stick to the protective method. We need not understand everything that happens when we meditate, although often we do later understand previous practice.

Asking for help. At times, however, a teacher's help makes practice more smooth and effective. This is particularly true during the rugged periods, those *vipassana* stages that correspond to the "dark nights" of St. John of the Cross. Prior to such times, you may also have questions about method that you want answered.

People sometimes feel that they should "back off" some in practice, fearing that they are getting in "too deep." Sometimes such a feeling needs to be honored, especially by those with a psychiatric history; often it is simply resistance. The situation can be explored with a teacher to arrive at the best decision.

If you feel you need help at any time, for any reason, you should ask for it. Be prepared to describe what happens in your sitting practice in some detail so that the teacher can diagnose your situation. Sometimes you may have fallen into faulty method, sometimes elaboration of a technique will help, and sometimes all you need is just patient persistence.

RES remains willing to help anyone who has learned awareness practice through it. A letter sent to the address given above will be answered. If you prefer telephone consultation, suggest the best time of day to call you. Please understand that RES must return calls collect. Ongoing guidance is also available for serious meditators who want it.

Choosing a teacher. Exercise some care when you choose an awareness practice teacher for either a retreat or continuing guidance. Most Eastern meditation forms have been refined over millennia by practitioners who took their work very seriously. The methods are quite powerful and have sound psychologies behind them. You want a teacher sufficiently knowledgeable and experienced to work with the method in your practice.

Customarily, people start teaching Eastern techniques when their own teacher feels they are ready. The potential teacher's personal practice should have ripened to a certain point, and he or she should also have sufficient conceptual understanding of the practice. Unfortunately, not everybody who offers to teach is truly prepared to do so. Some teach far too soon; some even teach without having been under the regular guidance of a teacher themselves.

Ask potential teachers several key questions. Find out if they have a teacher with whom they practice regularly. Ask how their teacher feels about their teaching. Find out if they

have someone to whom they can refer people whose practice is beyond their competence to guide. Notice carefully
how these questions are managed. Also observe which teachers live as you expect those committed to spiritual work
to live.

See how the teacher handles money and power relationships. Run in the opposite direction at any hint of sexual or
financial abuse of students. Nobody should get rich selling
spiritual teachings; this should be a red flag. Traditionally,
spiritual teachers do not ask for money for spiritual teachings. However, they can charge to cover travel expenses to
lead a retreat, the cost of students' room and board, and
incidental expenses incurred in putting on a retreat.

Look also to see if the focus is on the teachings or the person of the teacher. Good teachers do use examples from their
own lives and practice in their teaching; *how* they do so is the
issue. When a teacher is nearly worshiped or expects to be ex-
cessively revered by students, this is a warning signal. Good
teachers may be well spoken of by others but will discourage
any attempt to make themselves special.

Does the teacher promise you impossible things, such as
instant enlightenment or special powers? The only thing that
can safely be promised is hard work and progress in propor-
tion to that work. The focus should not be on enhancing the
ego, but on becoming selfless. If a teacher encourages much
talk about spiritual experiences, this probably supports ego-
ism. Beware also of a teacher who promises progress without
pointing out the need for a firm moral basis.

Working with a teacher. Teachers can be a great help
in spiritual practice. One who teaches a technique need not
be the only teacher you have. Other teachers can also help
you integrate spiritual living into your life as a whole. If you
work with any teacher, here are some guidelines to help you
profit most from it.

After choosing the teacher very carefully, adopt an obedi-
ent spirit regarding guidance. The teacher may not always be

right, and we should not be blind to striking error. However, often what we most dislike hearing is what we most need to hear. Having a truth-teller in your life is a great blessing. If we discard everything that is not agreeable to us, we are wasting both the teacher's and our own time. Keeping several teachers on tap to have one who yields to our whims in different situations is self-defeating.

Be completely honest. Sometimes what must be discussed with a teacher is uncomfortable, but this can be the cutting edge of growth. If we protect ego when meeting with a spiritual teacher, we cannot expect God to dissolve egocentricity for us. This does not mean that the teacher must know every trivial detail of your life; wanting that can itself be vanity. However, anything relevant to your working together should be shared.

Be grateful for what you are given. So many people lack opportunities for spiritual practice and guidance. Appreciate this real gift. Accept the limits of the relationship. Do not expect the spiritual teacher to function as a parent or best friend.

Finally, consult and listen to suitable spiritual teachers, but rely upon the teacher within. Put your spiritual practice and daily life in surrender to the purifying and sanctifying action of the Holy Spirit.

Integration into life. Here is some final food for thought. No matter what practice we do, how many teachers we consult, or whatever acts of surrender we make, our lives must reflect our commitment. We must willingly work on those areas of life and person where we can do something. We cannot expect God or the teacher to make magic for us. All of life must be lived in a way compatible with spiritual aspiration.

Let us look again at spiritual life as many spiritual giants have portrayed it. At the beginning, the work is mostly ours. We must do our part or nothing else will happen. In the middle, it is both God's and our work together that bring increasing purity. In the end, God will do it all. However, we must have done all that we can do earlier, and must have made ourselves completely docile to God's action. We can do no more important thing with our lives.

M.J.M.

NOTES

Chapter 1:
Purity of Heart:
The Teaching and Example of Jesus

1. Geoffrey W. Bromiley, *Theological Dictionary of the New Testament,* abridged in one volume (Grand Rapids, Mich.: William B. Eerdmans Publishing Company, 1985), 416.

2. *Dhammapada,* #236. The *Dhammapada* is available in many editions. To facilitate finding references in any edition, we cite by aphorism number.

Chapter 2:
The Buddhist Tradition of Insight Meditation

1. For a good translation, with commentary, see Nyanaponika Thera, *The Heart of Buddhist Meditation: A Handbook of Mental Training Based on the Buddhist Way of Mindfulness* (London: Rider Press, 1962).

2. The Pali Text Society has published many of these scriptures. Some may be obtained from Vihara Book Service, Washington, D.C., and some from Wisdom Publications, Boston.

3. Buddhaghosa, *The Path of Purification (Visuddhimagga),* translated from the Pali by Bhikkhu Nyanamoli (Kandy, Sri Lanka: Buddhist Publication Society, 1979).

4. Works available can be obtained through the Buddhist Publication Society, Sri Lanka, and the Vihara Book Service, Washington, D.C. A recent book by a foremost disciple of his is Venerable Sayadaw U Pandita, *In This Very Life: The Liberation Teachings of the Buddha* (Boston: Wisdom Publications, 1992).

5. Insight Meditation Society, 1230 Pleasant Street, Barre, MA 01005. You can write to get on the mailing list.

6. *The Experience of Insight: A Simple and Direct Guide to Buddhist Meditation*, 1983, *Seeking the Heart of Wisdom: The Path of Insight Meditation*, 1987, and *Insight Meditation: The Path to Freedom*, 1993, all published by Shambhala Press, Boston.

7. RES (Resources for Ecumenical Spirituality), P.O. Box 6, Mankato, MN 56002–0006 or RES, Route 1, Box 1160, Dunnegan, MO 65640–9705.

Chapter 3:
The Carmelite Tradition of Prayer

1. Teresa's classic definition of prayer is found in chapter 8 of the book of her *Life*: "For mental prayer in my opinion is nothing else than an intimate sharing between friends; it means taking time frequently to be alone with Him who we know loves us" (*Life*, 8:5). All further quotes from St. Teresa will be taken from *The Collected Works of St. Teresa of Avila*, trans. Kieran Kavanaugh, O.C.D., and Otilio Rodriguez, O.C.D., 3 vols. (Washington, D.C.: ICS Publications, 1976–85).

2. Teresa explains her early method of prayer as an effort to keep herself in the presence of Jesus Christ. "I tried as hard as I could to keep Jesus Christ, our God and Lord, present within me, and that was my way of prayer" (*Life*, 4:7). Teresa's method of prayer was not a discursive reflective one, but rather a psychological effort through faith and love to keep herself present to Christ living within her. She confesses in this same chapter and paragraph that she found difficulty with discursive meditation. Her way of prayer was simply to keep herself present through faith and love to the reality of Christ's presence within her.

3. In chapter 26 of *The Way of Perfection*, Teresa explains her prayer of recollection. This was her unique method of prayer and answer for those who, like herself, found difficulty with discursive meditation. It involves a recollecting of one's senses and directing one's attention lovingly within oneself to the Presence, the Reality of God within. Teresa explains to her readers that she is not asking them to think about Christ, but to "look at Him." To "look" at Christ means to remain present to the reality of Christ within our hearts. To "look" at Christ is an act of faith and love and does not necessarily mean imaging Christ with the imagination.

4. *Castle*, I, 1, 1. *Collected Works of St. Teresa*, vol. 2.

5. Actually, historians are uncertain about the exact date of John's birth. The closest date they come to is 1542. See *God Speaks in the Night: The Life, Times, and Teaching of St. John of the Cross* (Washington, D.C.: ICS Publications, 1991).

6. *The Dark Night*, book 1, chapter 10 par. 6, in *The Collected Works of St. John of the Cross*, rev. ed., trans. Kieran Kavanaugh, O.C.D. and Otilio Rodriguez, O.C.D. (Washington, D.C.: ICS Publications, 1991). See the note on citations of St. John of the Cross, above p. 20. In *The Living Flame of Love*, John uses the image of fire as a symbol of God's purifying love at work in contemplation.

7. A1, 13; A2, 7.

Chapter 4:
Christian Insight Meditation

1. Mary Jo Meadow and Kevin Culligan, "Congruent Spiritual Paths: Christian Carmelite and Theravadan Buddhist Vipassana," *Journal of Transpersonal Psychology* 19 (1987): 181–96.

2. Thomas Merton, *The Springs of Contemplation: A Retreat at the Abbey of Gethsemani*, ed. Jane Marie Richardson (New York: Farrar, Straus, Giroux, 1992), 177.

3. For a description in word and picture of a Christian Zen retreat, see Hugo M. Enomiya-Lassalle, *The Practice of Zen Meditation*, comp. and ed. Roland Ropers and Bogdan Snela, trans. Michelle Bromley (San Francisco: Aquarian Press, 1990).

4. Subsequently, they discovered that Denys Rackley, a Carthusian monk with extensive training in *vipassana*, had been offering insight meditation within three- and ten-day Christian retreats since 1982. His work is described in two articles in the *Boston Globe*: "A Carthusian Monk Reflects on Prayer and John Lennon," by James L. Franklin, January 14, 1983, and "An Eye on Eternity: A Priest Goes East in Search of His Soul," by Richard Higgins, December 17, 1990. In his retreats, Fr. Rackley presents *vipassana* in the context of selected New Testament themes that he explains in light of the meditation. The Silence and Awareness retreat presents insight meditation within the framework of John of the Cross's Christian spirituality.

Chapter 11:
Working with Auxiliary Practices: Walking and
Loving-Kindness Practices, Sharing Merit

1. This section teaches you how to do *metta* practice informally. You may want to learn more about it or how to make a full, formal practice of it. If so, see Mary Jo Meadow, *Gentling the Heart: Buddhist Loving-Kindness Practice for Christians* (New York: Crossroad, 1994).

Chapter 12:
St. John of the Cross:
Purification of Disordered Appetites

1. John's original Spanish in this third counsel uses the phrase *en su desprecio,* which Kavanaugh and Rodriguez translate literally as "contempt for yourself." I interpret this phrase more as non-attachment to self rather than contempt for self. Self-contempt, at least in our current English usage, connotes a pathological condition arising from negative conditioning in childhood and adolescence.

I do not believe John intends by this counsel to reinforce this negative attitude toward the self. At the same time, he very much wants us to act, speak, and think without inordinate attachment to ourselves and to desire that others do so also.

2. For a discussion of transformation of desire in John of the Cross, see Constance FitzGerald, O.C.D., *Spiritual Canticle as the Story of Human Desire: Its Development, Education, Purification, and Transformation,* four cassette audiotapes (Canfield, Ohio: Alba House Communications).

Chapter 13:
Teachings of the Buddha:
Purification of Conduct, the Gift of Morality

1. *Dhammapada,* #165.
2. Ibid., #342.
3. Ibid., #66, #69.
4. Ibid., #162–63.

5. Thich Nhat Hanh, *Interbeing: Commentaries on the Tiep Hien Precepts* (Berkeley, Calif.: Parallax Press, 1987), 51.

6. Ibid., 37.

7. Ibid., 45.

8. Ibid., 47.

9. Ibid., 54.

10. Ibid., 56.

11. Ibid., 57.

Chapter 16:
Teachings of the Buddha:
Purification of Mental Contents, Training the Mind

1. Thich Nhat Hanh, *Interbeing: Commentaries on the Tiep Hien Precepts* (Berkeley, Calif.: Parallax Press, 1987), 34.

2. If you want to learn *brahmavihara* practice in greater depth, see Mary Jo Meadow, *Gentling the Heart: Buddhist Loving-Kindness Practice for Christians* (New York: Crossroad, 1994).

3. *Dhammapada*, #5. The *Dhammapada* is available in many editions; to make finding references easy in any edition, we cite by aphorism number.

4. Nhat Hanh, *Interbeing*, 42.

5. Alan Watts, *The Wisdom of Insecurity* (New York: Pantheon Books, 1951), cited from 1968 paperback edition, p. 24.

6. Ibid.

7. Nhat Hanh, *Interbeing*, 39.

Chapter 18:
St. John of the Cross: Contemplative Purification

1. See A3, 35, 7; 36, 1–3; 37, 2; 43, 2; 44, 1–4.

Chapter 19:
Teachings of the Buddha: Purification
of the Heart — Wisdom, the Goal of Realization

1. Thich Nhat Hanh, *Interbeing: Commentaries on the Tiep Hien Precepts* (Berkeley, Calif.: Parallax Press, 1987), 27.

2. Ibid., 30.

3. Ibid., 32.

4. This appeared in a very early issue of the *National Catholic Reporter* newspaper.

5. Nhat Hanh, *Interbeing,* 49.

Chapter 21:
On Prayer, Meditation, and Contemplation

1. In St. Ignatius see, for example, the five "contemplations" on Jesus' Incarnation and Nativity during the first day of the Second Week in the Spiritual Exercises, in *Ignatius of Loyola: The Spiritual Exercises and Selected Works,* Classics of Western Spirituality, ed. George Ganss, S.J. (Mahwah, N.J.: Paulist Press, 1991), nos. 101-31, pp. 148-53; see also discussions of the terminology, pp. 61-63, 402 (no. 56). In St. John of the Cross, see N1, 10, 6; N1, 12, 4; N2, 5, 1; C13, 10; F3, 49.

2. Herbert Benson, *The Relaxation Response* (New York: William Morrow, 1975), 78-98.

Chapter 22:
On Jesus Christ and the Holy Spirit

1. See the "Sketch of Mount Carmel" in *The Collected Works of St. John of the Cross,* rev. ed., trans. Kieran Kavanaugh, O.C.D., and Otilio Rodriguez, O.C.D. (Washington, D.C.: ICS Publications, 1991), 110-11.

Chapter 23:
On Church Teachings

1. Pope John Paul II, "A Message of Hope to the Asian People," *Origins,* March 12, 1981, 611. Quoted in James A. Wiseman, "Christian Monastics and Interreligious Dialogue," *Cistercian Studies* 27 (1992): 258.

2. Vatican Congregation for the Doctrine of the Faith, "Some Aspects of Christian Meditation," *Origins,* December 28, 1989, 492-98.

3. Joseph Goldstein, *Insight Meditation: The Practice of Freedom* (Boston: Shambhala, 1993), 47.

4. *Origins,* December 28, 1989, 497, no. 12; also, *Acta Apostolicae Sedis,* 75 (March 1983): 256, and *Origins,* November 11, 1982, 359.

5. Pope John Paul II, "Beyond New Age Ideas: Spiritual Renewal," *Origins,* June 10, 1993, 59.

Chapter 24:
On Contemplative Prayer
and Doing Insight Practice

1. *Ascent of Mount Carmel,* book 2, chapters 12–15.

2. For a more detailed treatment of concentrative meditation practice, both management of problems and course of development, see Mary Jo Meadow, *Gentling the Heart: Buddhist Loving-Kindness Practice for Christians* (New York: Crossroad, 1994).

3. *Castle,* IV, 3, 11.

Chapter 25:
On Other Forms of Christian Prayer

1. Brother Lawrence of the Resurrection, *Writings and Conversations on the Practice of the Presence of God,* ed. Conrad De Meester, trans. Salvatore Sciurba (Washington, D.C.: ICS Publications, 1994), 98.

2. Herbert Benson (with William Proctor), *Your Maximum Mind* (New York: Avon Books, 1989), 24–47, 189–212.

Chapter 26:
On Carmelite Prayer

1. *Life,* 8:5. All quotes from St. Teresa are taken from *The Collected Works of St. Teresa of Avila,* trans. Kieran Kavanaugh and Otilio Rodriguez, 3 vols. (Washington, D.C.: ICS Publications, 1976–1985).

2. *Life,* 4:7.

3. *Life,* 9:6.

4. *Life,* 9:4. See also Jesús Castellano's enlightening discussion of Teresa's understanding of representing Christ in prayer in

"Teresa de Jesús nos enseña a orar," 125–26, from *Teresa de Jesús enseñanos a orar,* Tomás Alvarez and Jesús Castellano (Burgos: Editorial Monte Carmelo, 1982).

5. *Life,* 9:4.

6. *Way,* 29:7.

7. *Way,* 28:2.

8. *Way,* 28:4.

9. *Foundations,* 5:2.

10. *Castle,* IV, 1, 7.

11. For instance, John speaks of meditation in the following texts: A2, 15, 4–5; N1, 1, 1; F3, 32ff. This is not a complete list of his texts on meditation.

12. A2, 14, 2.

13. F3, 47.

14. F3, 29ff.

15. If we carefully follow John's discussion of the three blind guides in the third stanza of *The Living Flame of Love,* where he writes about the prayer of loving attention, we find that the prayer he suggests involves a process of self-emptying so that we may be receptive and disposed for the gift of contemplation. See F3:28–67.

16. In a fine study of St. John of the Cross, the Carmelite author Guido Stinissen maintains that the prayer of loving attention that John favors resembles "la meditation profonde" (meditation in depth, an emptying form of meditation). Stinissen maintains that those who practice Zen and other forms of depth meditation do not have to pass through the classical phase of movement from working with the intellect. What is needed for those who practice depth meditation is a deepening of faith so that their prayer does not become a vague religious sentiment, but rather a true personal encounter with God. See Guido Stinissen, *Decouvre-moi ta presence: recontres avec Saint Jean de la Croix* (Paris: Editions du Cerf, 1989).

Chapter 27:
On Psychological Factors in Meditation

1. *Way,* 19:9.

2. *Castle,* IV, 2, 1.

Chapter 28:
On Getting Guidance in Practice

1. The Culligan-Meadow workshop on spiritual direction is in press. Meadow's tapes are: *Torments of the Mind: Our Darker Side, Faith and Knowing God,* and *Spiritual Hunger: Choosing Your Joy.*

BIBLIOGRAPHY

Abbott, Walter M., ed. *The Documents of Vatican II*. New York: America Press, 1966.

Barnes, Michael. "Theological Trends: The Buddhist-Christian Dialogue." *The Way* (England) 30 (1990): 55–64.

Benson, Herbert. *The Relaxation Response*. New York: William Morrow, 1975.

———. *Your Maximum Mind*. With William Proctor. New York: Avon Books, 1989.

Bromiley, Geoffrey W. *Theological Dictionary of the New Testament*. Abridged in one volume. Grand Rapids, Mich.: William B. Eerdmans Publishing Co., 1985.

Buddhaghosa. *The Path of Purification (Visuddhimagga)*. Trans. Bhikkhu Nyanamoli. Kandy, Sri Lanka: Buddhist Publication Society, 1979.

Castellano, Jesús. "Teresa de Jesús nos ensña a orar." In Tomás Alvarez and Jesús Castellano, *Teresa de Jesús enséñanos a orar*. Burgos: Editorial Monte Carmelo, 1982.

Chowning, Daniel, Kevin Culligan, and Mary Jo Meadow. *Silence and Awareness: A Retreat Experience in Christian-Buddhist Meditation*. Twelve cassette audiotapes. Kansas City, Mo. Credence Cassettes.

Culligan, Kevin, and Mary Jo Meadow. *Nobody Walks Alone: Spiritual Guidance in the Carmelite Tradition*. Audiocassette program. Kansas City, Mo.: Credence Cassettes, forthcoming.

Dhammapada, The. Available in and cited from various translations and editions. One readily available is translated by Juan Mascaró. New York: Penguin Books, 1973.

Enomiya-Lassalle, Hugo M. *The Practice of Zen Meditation*. Comp. and ed. Roland Ropers and Bogdan Snela. Trans. Michelle Bromley. San Francisco, The Aquarian Press, 1990.

Farrelly, John. "Notes on Mysticism in Today's World." *Spirituality Today* 43 (1991): 104–18.

FitzGerald, Constance. *Spiritual Canticle as the Story of Human Desire: Its Development, Education, Purification, and Transformation*. Four cassette audiotapes. Canfield, Ohio: Alba House Communications.

Franklin, James L. "A Carthusian Reflects on Prayer and John Lennon." *Boston Globe*, January 14, 1983.

Freeman, Laurence. "Meditation." In *The New Dictionary of Catholic Spirituality.* Ed. Michael Downey. A Michael Glazier Book. Collegeville, Minn.: Liturgical Press, 1993. 648–51.

Goldstein, Joseph. *The Experience of Insight: A Simple and Direct Guide to Buddhist Meditation.* Boston: Shambhala Publications, 1987.

———. *Insight Meditation: The Practice of Freedom.* Boston: Shambhala Publications, 1993.

Goldstein, Joseph, and Jack Kornfield. *Seeking the Heart of Wisdom: The Path of Insight Meditation.* Boston: Shambhala Publications, 1987.

Higgins, Richard. "An Eye on Eternity: A Priest Goes East in Search of His Soul." *Boston Globe,* December 17, 1990.

Ignatius of Loyola. *The Spiritual Exercises and Selected Works.* Ed. George Ganss. Classics of Western Spirituality. Mahwah, N.J.: Paulist Press, 1991.

John of the Cross, St. *The Collected Works.* Rev. ed. Trans. Kieran Kavanaugh and Otilio Rodriguez. Washington, D.C.: ICS Publications, 1991.

John Paul II, Pope. "A Message of Hope to the Asian People." *Origins,* March 12, 1981, 611.

———. "Teresa of Avila: God's Vagabond." *Origins,* November 11, 1982, 358–60

———. "Beyond New Age Ideas: Spiritual Renewal." *Origins,* June 10, 1993, 59–61.

Lawrence of the Resurrection, Brother. *Writings and Conversations on the Practice of the Presence of God.* Critical Edition by Conrad De Meester. Trans. Salvatore Sciurba. Washington, D.C.: ICS Publications, 1994.

LeShan, Lawrence. *How to Meditate: A Guide to Self-Discovery.* New York: Bantam Books, 1975.

Meadow, Mary Jo, and Kevin Culligan. "Congruent Spiritual Paths: Christian Carmelite and Theravadan Buddhist Vipassana." *Journal of Transpersonal Psychology* 19 (1987): 181–96.

Meadow, Mary Jo. *Gentling the Heart: Buddhist Loving-Kindness Practice for Christians.* New York: Crossroad, 1994.

———. *Faith and Knowing God.* Cassette audiotape. Kansas City, Mo., Credence Cassettes.

Spiritual Hunger: Choosing Your Joy. Cassette audiotape. Kansas City, Mo., Credence Cassettes.

———. *Torments of the Mind: Our Darker Side.* Cassette audiotape. Kansas City, Mo., Credence Cassettes.

Merton, Thomas. *The Springs of Contemplation: A Retreat at the Abbey of Gethsemani.* Ed. Jane Marie Richardson. New York: Farrar, Straus, Giroux, 1992.

Nhat Hanh, Thich. *Interbeing: Commentaries on the Tiep Hien Precepts.* Berkeley, Calif.: Parallax Press, 1987.

Nyanaponika, Thera. *The Heart of Buddhist Meditation: A Handbook of Mental Training Based on the Buddhist Way of Mindfulness.* London: Rider Press, 1962.

O'Hanlon, Daniel J. "Integration of Spiritual Practices: A Western Christian Looks East." *Journal of Transpersonal Psychology* 13 (1981): 91–112.

Rahula, Walpola. *What the Buddha Taught.* Rev. ed. New York: Grove Weidenfeld, 1974.

Ruiz, Federico, et al. *God Speaks in the Night: The Life, Times, and Teaching of St. John of the Cross.* Trans. Kieran Kavanaugh. Washington, D.C.: ICS Publications, 1991.

Sayadaw, U Pandita. *In This Very Life: The Liberation Teachings of the Buddha.* Boston: Wisdom Publications, 1992.

Stinissen, Guido. *Decouvre-moi ta presence: recontres avec Saint Jean de la Croix.* Paris: Editions du Cerf, 1989.

Teasdale, Wayne. "Interreligious Dialogue since Vatican II: The Monastic-Contemplative Dimension." *Spirituality Today* 43 (1991): 119–33.

Teresa of Avila, St. *The Collected Works.* Trans. Kieran Kavanaugh and Otilio Rodriguez. 3 vols. Washington, D.C.: ICS Publications, 1976–1985.

Vatican Congregation for the Doctrine of the Faith. "Letter to the Bishops of the Catholic Church on Some Aspects of Christian Meditation." *Origins,* December 28, 1989, 492–98.

Watts, Alan. *The Wisdom of Insecurity.* New York: Pantheon Books, 1951; paperback ed., 1968.

Wiseman, James A. "Christian Monastics and Interreligious Dialogue." *Cistercian Studies* 27 (1992): 257–71.